The Art of Mushroom Cultivation

The Home Gardener's Guide to Mushroom Cultivation: Learn to Identify, Cultivate, and Enjoy Everything You Need for Growing Gourmet and Medicinal Mushrooms

By
Maxwell Mamyco

Copyrighted Material

© **Copyright 2023 - All rights reserved**

The content contained within this book may not be reproduced, duplicated, or transmitted without direct written permission from the author or the publisher.

Under no circumstances will any blame or legal responsibility be held against the publisher, or author, for any damages, reparation, or monetary loss due to the information contained within this book. Either directly or indirectly.

Legal Notice:

This book is copyright protected. This book is only for personal use. You cannot amend, distribute, sell, use, quote, or paraphrase any part, or the content within this book, without the consent of the author or publisher.

Disclaimer Notice

Please note the information contained within this document is for educational and entertainment purposes only. All effort has been executed to present accurate, up-to-date, and reliable, complete information. No warranties of any kind are declared or implied. Readers acknowledge that the author is not engaging in the rendering of legal, financial, medical, or professional advice. The content within this book has been derived from various sources. Please consult a licensed professional before attempting any techniques outlined in this book.

By reading this document, the reader agrees that under no circumstances is the author responsible for any losses, direct or indirect, which are incurred as a result of the use of the information contained within this document, including, but not limited to, — errors, omissions, or inaccuracies.

Table of Contents

PART I: Fundamentals of Mushrooms and Their Cultivation 8

Introduction 8

- The Healing Harvest - Medicinal Power of Mushrooms 9
  - Immune Support 9
  - Antioxidant Properties 9
- Cultivation of Mushrooms 10
  - Choosing the Right Mushroom Species 10
  - Required Materials and Equipment 10
  - Methods of Cultivation 10
- Using Mushrooms in Dish Preparation 11
  - Basic Preparation Techniques 11
- Nutritional Value of Mushrooms 12
  - Vitamins and Minerals 12
  - Dietary Fiber 12
  - Low in Calories and Fat 12

Chapter 1: Different Types of Mushrooms 13

- Different type of mushroom 13
- Identification of Mushrooms 13
  - Mushroom Anatomy 13
  - Field Guides and Expert Advice 14
- Characteristics of Different Types of Mushrooms 14
  - Gilled Mushrooms 14
  - Boletes 15
  - Polypores 15
  - Coral and Club Fungi 15
  - Puffballs and Earthstars 15
- Recognizing Edible and Toxic Mushrooms 15
  - Edible Mushrooms 15
  - Toxic Mushrooms 16
- How to Identify and Discard Toxic Mushrooms 16
  - Learn the "Dangerous Lookalikes" 16
  - Use Multiple Identification Methods 17
  - When in Doubt, Throw It Out 17
  - Know Your Local Species 17
- An Overview of Mushroom Families 17
  - Agaricaceae 17
  - Boletaceae 17
  - Russulaceae 18
  - Cantharellaceae 18
  - Morchellaceae 18
- The Importance of Fungi to the Environment 18
  - Decomposition 18
  - The Relationships of Mycorrhizal Fungi 19
  - Germs That Cause Disease and Illness 19
- Tips and Guidelines for Mushroom Hunting in the Wild 19
  - Obtain Permission and Follow Regulations 19
  - Practice Responsible Foraging 19

- Be Ready for Anything and Keep Yourself Safe 20
- Methods for the Conservation and Stockpiling of Mushrooms 20
  - Housekeeping 20
  - Methods for the Storage of Fresh Mushrooms 20
  - Drying 21
  - Freezing 21
- The Medicinal Properties of Mushrooms 21
  - Ganoderma lucidum (Reishi) 21
  - Lentinula edodes (shiitake) 21
  - Grifola frondosa (Maitake) 22
  - Hericium erinaceus, "Lion's Mane." 22
  - Turkey Tail (Trametes versicolor) 22
- Benefits of Consuming Medicinal Mushrooms as Part of Your Diet 22
- The Importance of Mycology in Today's Scientific Community 22
  - Research in the Field of Medicine 22
  - Agriculture and Pest Control 23
  - Environmental Cleanup and Restoration Work 23

Chapter 2: Different Substrates for Mushroom Cultivation 24

- Common Substrates for Mushroom Cultivation 25
  - Straw 25
  - Sawdust 25
  - Wood Logs 25
  - Compost 25
  - Grain 26
- Preparing Substrates for Mushroom Cultivation 26
  - Hydration 26
  - Sterilization or Pasteurization 26
  - The Process of Inoculation and Cooling 26
- Humidity, Temperature, and Light Requirements for Mushroom Growth 27
  - Humidity 27
  - Temperature 27
  - Light 27
- Mushroom Cultivation Techniques 28
  - The Method of Using a Bag 28
  - The Method of Using a Tray or Tub 28
  - The Method of the Bottle 28
  - Application of the Log Method 29
  - The Method of Using an Outdoor Bed 29
- Factors to Consider When Choosing a Mushroom Cultivation Technique 29
  - Mushroom Species 29
  - Available Space 30
  - Financial Plan and Available Means 30
  - Experience Level 30
- Advanced Techniques and Tips for Mushroom Cultivation 30
  - Optimizing Substrate Composition 30
  - Nitrogen Content 31
  - The Relationship Between Carbon and Nitrogen 31
  - Mineral Content 31
- Enhancing the Existing Conditions of the Environment 32
  - Automated Control of the Relative Humidity 32
  - Temperature Control 32
  - The Regulation of the Light 32

- Advanced Cultivation Techniques 33
  - Liquid Culture Inoculation 33
  - Cloning Wild Mushrooms 33
  - Environmental Manipulation 33
- Common Solutions to Problems Encountered in Mushroom Cultivation 34
  - Suppress the Growth of the Mycelium 34
  - Poor Fruiting or Low Yields 34
  - Contamination 34

Chapter 3: Pasteurization and Inoculation in Mushroom Cultivation 36

- Pasteurization in Mushroom Cultivation 37
  - Common Pasteurization Methods 37
- Inoculation in Mushroom Cultivation 39
  - Popular Inoculation Methods 39
- Monitoring and Optimizing the Growth Environment 41
  - Temperature 41
  - Humidity 41
  - Light 42
  - Air Exchange 43
- Common Solutions to Problems Encountered in Mushroom Cultivation 44
  - Contamination 44
  - Mycelial Growth That Is Sluggish or Completely Stopped 44
  - Poor Fruiting or Yield 45
  - Mushroom Development That Is Abnormal or Malformed 45

Chapter 4: Mushroom Cultivation from Spores or Mycelium 47

- Spores vs. Mycelium 48
  - Spores 48
  - Mycelium 48
- Varieties of Methods Used in Cultivation 48
  - Bottle Culture 48
  - Bag Culture 49
  - Substrate Culture 49
- Essential Items for a Successful Mushroom Farming Operation 50
  - Equipment Used for the Processes of Sterilization and Pasteurization 50
  - Instruments and Supplies for Inoculation 50
  - Containers 51
  - Environmental Control Equipment 51
- Procedures to Follow When Growing Mushrooms from Their Spores and Mycelium 51
  - Preparation 51
  - The immunization 52
  - The Incubation Period 53
  - Fruiting 54
  - Harvesting 55
  - Care and Storage Following the Harvest 55

PART II: Harvesting and Culinary Use of Mushrooms 57

Chapter 5: Signs of Mushroom Maturity 57

- Signs of Mushroom Maturity 57
  - Cap Development 58
  - Veil Breakage 58

- Spore Release 58
- Methods for the Harvesting of Mushrooms 58
  - Preparing for Harvest 59
  - Gentle Twisting and Pulling 59
  - Using a Knife or Scissors to Cut Something 59
  - Care and Storage Following the Harvest 59
- Safety Measures to Take During the Harvest 60
  - Sterile Environment 60
  - Timetable for the Harvest 60
  - Exercise Caution When Working with Mushrooms 60
- Reaping the Benefits of Several Flushes 60
  - Rest Period 61
  - Repletion of Fluids 61
  - Oversight and Maintenance of the System 61
- Methods of Harvesting Requisite for Individual Species of Mushrooms 61
  - Agaricus bisporus (White Button Mushroom) 62
  - Pleurotus ostreatus (Oyster Mushroom) 62
  - Lentinula edodes (shiitake mushroom) 62
- Common Harvesting Issues and How to Troubleshoot Them 63
  - Mushrooms that Do Not Mature or Grow at A Snail's Pace 63
  - Cracking or Splitting of the Capsules of Mushrooms 63
  - Fungi that Have Been Infested by Insects or Other Pests 64
  - Possible Contamination with Mold or Bacteria 64
- Post-Harvest Handling and Storage 64
  - Cleaning and Preserving Mushrooms 64
  - The Process of Drying Mushrooms 64
  - Methods for the Storage of Fresh Mushrooms 65

Chapter 6: Most Commonly Cultivated Mushrooms for Gastronomy 66

- Wild Cultivable Mushrooms 67
  - Morel (Morchella spp.) 67
  - Chanterelle (Cantharellus spp.) 67
  - Porcini (Boletus edulis) 67
- Exotic Mushrooms 67
  - Enoki (Flammulina velutipes) 68
  - Lion's Mane (Hericium erinaceus) 68
  - Black Trumpet (Craterellus cornucopioides) 68
  - Shiitake (Lentinula edodes) 68
  - Oyster (Pleurotus spp.) 69
- The Flavor and the Nutritional Benefits of Edible Mushrooms 69
  - Vitamins 69
  - Minerals 69
  - Protein and Fiber 70
  - Antioxidants in Addition to Other Benefits to Health 70
- Growing Edible Mushrooms in the Comfort of Your Own Home 70
  - Selecting the Appropriate Species of Mushroom 70
  - Choosing the Most Appropriate Cultivation Medium 70
  - Establishing the Optimal Conditions for Plant Growth 71
  - Inoculation and Colonization 71
  - The Process of Bearing Fruit and Harvesting 71
- Common Solutions to Problems Encountered in Mushroom Cultivation 71
  - Contamination 72
  - Poor fruiting 72

  Growth That Is Irregular or Sluggish 72
 Methods for the Preservation and Storage of Edible Mushrooms 72
  Evaporation 72
  Freezing 73
  Putting in Cans 73
  Pickling 73
 Enjoying Your Homegrown Gastronomic Mushrooms 74

Bonus Chapter: Mushroom-Based Recipes 75

 Main Dishes 76
  Mushroom Risotto 76
  Mushroom Pasta 77
  Mushroom Stew 79
  Mushroom-Stuffed Bell Peppers 80
  Mushroom and Spinach Lasagna 82
 Side Dishes 83
  Grilled Mushrooms 84
  Sautéed Mushrooms 85
  Roasted Mushrooms 86
  Garlic and Herb Stuffed Mushrooms 87
  Balsamic Glazed Mushrooms 88
 Desserts 89
  Chocolate-Coated Mushrooms 89
  Mushroom Pie 90
  Mushroom and Walnut Tart 92
  Mushroom and Fig Bread Pudding 93
  Chocolate and Mushroom Mousse 94

PART III: Medicinal Use and Preservation of Mushrooms 97

Chapter 7: Mushrooms Used in Traditional Medicine 97

 Therapeutic Properties of Medicinal Mushrooms 97
 Cultivation of Medicinal Mushrooms 98
  Cultivating Reishi Mushrooms 99
  Cultivating Cordyceps Mushrooms 99
  Cultivating Shiitake and Maitake Mushrooms 100
 Culinary Preparation of Medicinal Mushrooms 101

Chapter 8: Techniques for Preserving and Storing Fresh Mushrooms 103

 Drying Techniques for Mushrooms 103
  Air Drying 104
  Oven Drying 104
  Dehydrator Drying 105
 Freezing Techniques for Mushrooms 105
  Blanching and Freezing 106
  Flash Freezing 106
 Storage Tips for Fresh Mushrooms 107
 Storing Dried Mushrooms 108
 Storing Frozen Mushrooms 108

Conclusion 110

PART I: Fundamentals of Mushrooms and Their Cultivation

Introduction

Mushrooms, those uniquely appealing and complex organisms that nestle on forest floors and speckle the edges of our backyard gardens, have long been subjects of fascination, fear, and of course, culinary delight. Enveloping the reader into this often unexplored world, our book, ***"The Art of Mushroom Cultivation"*** is an all-in-one guide designed to transform the amateur mycologist or culinary enthusiast into a seasoned mushroom cultivator and gourmand. Offering you a chance to grow your own mushrooms at home and master the art of incorporating them into your meals, this book is your indispensable companion in a journey that's as educational as it is exciting.

Firstly, the book is your portal to discover the world of mushroom cultivation. Mushrooms are extraordinary organisms, falling neither into the category of plant nor animal, and have a cultivation process that's entirely unique. Our book thoroughly details this process, from understanding the mushroom life cycle to selecting the right species for growth. It lays out the requisite materials and equipment, and offers step-by-step methods for successful cultivation. The reader will not only grow mushrooms but will understand them, gaining a comprehensive knowledge of their life from spore to mature fungus.

The Healing Harvest - Medicinal Power of Mushrooms

What is also unique about this book is its keen emphasis on the medicinal properties of mushrooms. Known as nature's healing gifts, mushrooms are rich in therapeutic properties, from anti-inflammatory attributes to cognitive health benefits. Each species has its unique properties, and learning about these can lead you on the path to a healthier lifestyle. Not only do we delve into the well-known health benefits of widely consumed mushrooms, but we also shine light on less common species known for their therapeutic properties. By cultivating these species at home, you will have easy access to their health benefits.

For their beneficial effects on human health, mushrooms have been used in traditional Chinese medicine for a very long time. Mushrooms have become even more popular as a result of their ability to enhance general well-being, and contemporary scientific evidence is helping to back up these claims.

Immune Support

It has been shown that beta-glucans, a specific form of complex carbohydrate that is found in a variety of mushrooms, including shiitake, maitake, and turkey tail, are beneficial to the immune system. According to a number of studies, these chemicals may assist in the regulation of immune cells, possibly enhancing the body's capacity to ward off illnesses and infections.

Antioxidant Properties

In addition, mushrooms have a high concentration of antioxidants, which are known to assist the body in its fight against free radicals. Free radicals are molecules that are unstable and have the ability to cause damage to cells, which may then possibly lead to a variety of health problems such as cancer and heart disease. Consuming foods high in antioxidants, such as mushrooms, may assist in lowering the chance of developing certain illnesses.

Cultivation of Mushrooms

The Mushroom Life Cycle

It is necessary to have an understanding of the life cycle of mushrooms in order to successfully cultivate these extraordinary creatures. Mycelium is a network of thread-like structures that develop inside a substrate. The process starts with the formation of spores, which germinate to produce mycelium. Once the mycelium has developed to its full potential, it will produce a fruiting body, which is more often referred to as a mushroom. This fruiting body is responsible for dispersing spores, which initiate a new cycle.

Choosing the Right Mushroom Species

When starting out in mushroom cultivation, it is essential to choose the correct species of mushroom to grow. White button mushrooms, oyster mushrooms, and shiitake mushrooms are three varieties of fungi that are often grown in home gardens. Because they are often simpler to cultivate, these species are a wonderful option for those who are just starting out in the world of mushroom farming.

Required Materials and Equipment

You will need particular ingredients and equipment in order to properly develop mushrooms. These include a growing medium, spores or spawn, containers, and a climate that is conducive to growth. These components will be different for you to use based on the species of mushroom you opt to cultivate and the technique of growth that you go with.

Methods of Cultivation

There are a few different approaches to growing mushrooms, and each one comes with its own set of benefits and difficulties. The following is a list of some of the more common methods for growing mushrooms at home

The PF-Tek Method

Growing mushrooms in tiny jars that are filled with a substrate combination that typically consists of brown rice flour, vermiculite, and water is the approach that is used in the PF Tek (PsilocybeFanaticus Technique), which is a method that is both straightforward and economical. This procedure is easy to follow, even for novices, and it produces successful results with fungi such as oysters and white button mushrooms.

Straw Cultivation

Mushrooms, notably oyster mushrooms, may be grown using straw as the substrate in a process known as "straw cultivation," which entails utilizing a sterilized straw. After being heated and sterilized, the straw is further injected with mushroom spawn before being packaged in bags or other containers. Mycelium spreads throughout the straw and finally produces fruiting bodies in the form of mushrooms.

Wood-Based Cultivation

Mushrooms like shiitake and maitake do well when grown on hardwood logs or sawdust, which are both byproducts of wood production and are suitable for cultivating these species. To grow mushrooms using this technique, you first sterilize hardwood logs or sawdust blocks, then inoculate them with mushroom spawn, and then let the mycelium colonize the substrate.

Liquid Culture Technique

The liquid culture approach includes cultivating mycelium in a nutrient-rich liquid solution. When the mycelium has reached the appropriate size, it may be transplanted onto a substrate to begin the process of producing fruiting bodies. This procedure is more complex than others, and it must be carried out under sterile working conditions; nonetheless, it may lead to quicker colonization periods.

Using Mushrooms in Dish Preparation

Basic Preparation Techniques

It is vital to have a working knowledge of fundamental preparation skills before adding mushrooms to any of your recipes. These techniques include cleaning, trimming, and slicing the mushrooms. If you take the time to thoroughly clean and handle your mushrooms, you may improve both their taste and their consistency, making them an even tastier complement to any recipe.

Cooking Methods

Cooking mushrooms may be done in a variety of ways, including stir-frying, roasting, grilling, and sautéing. Some of these techniques are included below. The mushrooms take on a distinct taste and texture depending on the preparation technique, which enables them to complement and enhance a variety of cuisines.

Recipe Ideas

Mushrooms are versatile ingredients that may be used in a broad variety of dishes, ranging from simple starters to complex main meals. Dishes like mushroom risotto, mushroom-filled mushrooms, mushroom soup, and mushroom stroganoff are among the most common uses of mushrooms. Because of the many uses to which they may be put, they are an invaluable addition to any cooking space.

Nutritional Value of Mushrooms

Vitamins and Minerals

Mushrooms are a fantastic resource for a wide variety of important vitamins and minerals, such as vitamins B2, B3, B5, and D, in addition to selenium, copper, and potassium. These nutrients are very important to the upkeep and preservation of one's general health and well-being.

Dietary Fiber

In addition, mushrooms are an excellent source of dietary fiber that facilitates digestion and contributes to the maintenance of a healthy weight. A decreased total cholesterol level and a reduced likelihood of developing coronary heart disease are two potential benefits of eating a diet high in fiber.

Low in Calories and Fat

Because of their low calorie and fat content, mushrooms are an excellent food choice for anyone on a diet. As a result of their ability to enhance the taste and consistency of meals without contributing an excessive number of calories, they are an excellent component for those who are interested in leading healthy lifestyles.

Chapter 1: Different Types of Mushrooms

Different type of mushroom

Since the beginning of human history, people have been fascinated with mushrooms since they belong to a wide collection of fungi that are quite interesting. They are very important to the ecosystem as a result of their work in decomposing organic materials and recycling nutrients. In addition to their significance in the culinary and medical arts, mushrooms are widely prized for their aesthetic appeal. In this chapter, we will discuss the many different kinds of mushrooms, how to identify them and their features, how to distinguish edible mushrooms from dangerous mushrooms, and the significance of proper identification for the purpose of ensuring the safety of ingestion.

Identification of Mushrooms

Mushroom Anatomy

In order to correctly identify a mushroom, it is necessary to have a fundamental understanding of its anatomy. The following is a rundown of the main components of a regular mushroom:

- The structure that looks like an umbrella and forms the top of the mushroom is called the cap or pileus.
- The way it is shaped, the color it is, and the texture it has may all help identify it.
- Gills, also known as lamellae, are structures that resemble thin blades and are located on the underside of the cap. They may be widely separated or narrowly spaced, and the hue can change between the two.
- The central column that supports the cap is referred to as the stem or the stipe. The term "annulus" refers to a ring- or skirt-like structure that may or may not be present on the stem of a plant. Stems may be either short or long, thick or thin.
- The spore print is a critical identifying tool that may be generated by putting the cap on a sheet of paper and letting the spores fall onto the surface of the paper. When trying to accurately identify a spore print, the color and pattern of the print may be quite important.

Field Guides and Expert Advice

When one is trying to learn how to recognize different kinds of mushrooms, it is very necessary to study reliable field guides or online resources that provide in-depth information on the appearance, habitat, and seasonality of various mushroom species. It is also vital to seek advice from seasoned mycologists or to join local mycological groups in order to gain knowledge from the expertise of other individuals in the field.

Characteristics of Different Types of Mushrooms

There are hundreds of different kinds of mushrooms on the globe, each with its own unique appearance, including size, color, and texture. The following is a list of some general classifications of mushrooms that are based on their characteristics:

Gilled Mushrooms

The presence of gills on the underside of the cap distinguishes this form of mushroom from all others. It is also the most common species of mushroom. Agaricus, also known as the white button mushroom; Amanita, which includes the potentially lethal Amanita phalloides; and Lactarius, often known as the milk cap mushroom, are among examples.

Boletes

On the underside of the cap, where gills would normally be, boletes have holes instead. These mushrooms are often rather huge and thick, and they have a stem running through the middle of them. Boletus edulis, also known as porcini, and Suillus, sometimes known as slippery jacks, are two well-known examples.

Polypores

Polypores are a kind of bracket fungus that may be seen growing on trees or logs that have fallen down. They have a grain that is similar to that of leather, and the underside of the cap has pores. Examples include Ganoderma lucidum (reishi) and Fomes fomentarius.

Coral and Club Fungi

Coral fungi are those that have structures that look like branching coral, while club fungi have projections that look like clubs or fingers. Both kinds are missing a cap and a stem in their typical forms. Examples include Ramaria (a coral fungus) and Clavariadelphus (a club fungus).

Puffballs and Earthstars

When they have reached maturity, puffball fungi, which may be spherical or pear-shaped, discharge their spores via a narrow aperture. Earthstars are fungi that look very much like puffballs but have an outer covering in the form of a star that may split apart to expose the spore sac. There is the Lycoperdon, also known as the puffball, and the Geastrum, also known as the earthstar.

Recognizing Edible and Toxic Mushrooms

Edible Mushrooms

Both their taste and their contribution to one's diet make edible mushrooms quite desirable.

The following are examples of well-known food species:

- The Agaricusbisporus, most often known as the "white button mushroom,"
- Pleurotusostreatus (oyster mushroom)
- Morchella esculenta (morel)
- Chanterelle, scientific name: Cantharellus cibarius

- Boletus edulis (porcini)
- It is vital to note that even edible mushrooms may trigger allergic responses or pain in the gastrointestinal tract in some people, which is why it is necessary to eat new species in moderate quantities at first.

Toxic Mushrooms

The consumption of toxic mushrooms may result in a wide variety of symptoms, ranging from a simple upset stomach to serious organ failure and even death. The need for thorough identification arises from the fact that many poisonous mushroom species superficially resemble edible varieties. The following are some examples of species that should be avoided:

- The Amanita phalloides mushroom, sometimes known as the "death cap," is notoriously lethal and is the cause of the vast majority of fatal mushroom poisonings worldwide.
- The Amanita muscaria mushroom, also known as the fly agaric, is responsible for hallucinations, nausea, and other symptoms. The red cap with white spots that this fungus has can help you identify it.
- Galerina marginata, often known as deadly galerina, is a little brown mushroom that, like the death cap, is poisonous due to the presence of fatal toxins.
- Species belonging to the genus Cortinarius: Some of the species in this genus generate a poison known as orellanine that is capable of causing renal failure.

How to Identify and Discard Toxic Mushrooms

Learn the "Dangerous Lookalikes"

While it is important to learn to recognize edible mushrooms, it is also important to be aware of the potentially harmful mushrooms that closely mimic them. For instance, the edible Agaricus campestris, sometimes known as the meadow mushroom, is readily mistaken for members of the poisonous Amanita genus. It is important to educate oneself on the distinctions between edible and poisonous plants and to reference authoritative resources in order to avoid being confused.

Use Multiple Identification Methods

Confirming the identity of a mushroom requires the use of a number of different identification techniques, including spore prints, habitat, seasonality, and other distinctive traits. It's best not to base your identification just on a single trait, such as color or form, since these aspects might change within a species or mislead you.

When in Doubt, Throw It Out

If you are unable to positively identify a mushroom, the safest course of action is to err on the side of caution and throw it away. It is not worth the chance of being poisoned or having an adverse reaction if you consume mushrooms that you are unsure about.

Know Your Local Species

Get to know the common edible and poisonous mushrooms that grow in your region so you can avoid them. This will assist you in recognizing species that pose a risk to your health and enable you to make better-educated choices on the types of mushrooms to harvest and eat.

An Overview of Mushroom Families

It is vital to become well-versed in the primary mushroom families in order to make progress in one's exploration of the world of mushrooms. This will offer a good basis for learning the many qualities of each of them as well as accurately recognizing them.

Agaricaceae

The family Agaricaceae is home to a wide variety of mushrooms, some of which are well-known, such as the white button mushroom (Agaricus bisporus) and the species of the toxic genus Amanita. In general, mushrooms belonging to this family have a cap and a stem, and their gills are located beneath. They differ widely in size, color, and whether or not they can be consumed, making proper identification very necessary.

Boletaceae

On the underside of the cap, Boletaceae mushrooms have holes rather than gills, which is one of the characteristics that distinguish them. This family of mushrooms includes a number of edible species, such as the highly sought-after porcini (Boletus edulis) and the king bolete (Boletus edulis var. grandedulis). Nevertheless, there are members of this family that might cause discomfort in the gastrointestinal tract; therefore, correct identification is required.

Russulaceae

The mushrooms belonging to the Russulaceae family are recognized for having a texture that is crumbly and brittle. This family includes the genera Russula and Lactarius. They create mycorrhizal associations with the trees that they find in their natural habitat, which is often a forest setting. Although there are many edible species, there are also those that might cause gastrointestinal distress and a few that are hazardous.

Cantharellaceae

Both the chanterelle (Cantharellus cibarius) and the black trumpet (Craterellus cornucopioides) belong to the family Cantharellaceae. Chanterelles are very popular mushrooms. The caps of these mushrooms have a characteristic funnel form, and the undersides of their stems are ridged in a manner that resembles gills. The majority of the species in this family are known to be both edible and delectable.

Morchellaceae

The renowned morels (Morchella spp.), which are members of the Morchellaceae family of mushrooms, are highly regarded for their distinctive honeycomb-like appearance as well as their delicious taste. When properly prepared, morels may be eaten; however, the raw mushroom should never be swallowed since it contains a toxin that can irritate the gastrointestinal tract.

The Importance of Fungi to the Environment

Fungi, which are the organisms that produce mushrooms, are critical to the upkeep of ecosystems all around the globe. Mushrooms are the fruiting bodies of fungi. Fungi are responsible for a variety of important tasks, including the following:

Decomposition

Fungal decomposition is the process by which dead plant and animal matter are returned to the soil after being broken down. This procedure is essential for preserving the fertility of the soil and fostering the development of plants.

The Relationships of Mycorrhizal Fungi

Mycorrhizae are the symbiotic associations that many species of fungus create with the roots of plants. The plant offers the fungal carbohydrates that were created via photosynthesis in exchange for the fungi's assistance in the plant's ability to better absorb nutrients and water from the soil.

Germs That Cause Disease and Illness

Certain types of fungi may act as pathogens and spread illness to other organisms, including people, animals, and plants. Despite the fact that these fungi might have a detrimental influence, they are important for ecosystems because they help regulate populations and keep the environment in balance.

Tips and Guidelines for Mushroom Hunting in the Wild

Foraging for mushrooms is an activity that may be lucrative and fun, but it is vital to follow best practices in order to guarantee safety for the forager as well as the environment.

Obtain Permission and Follow Regulations

If you want to forage on private property, you should always get permission beforehand, and you should be aware of any local rules governing the collection of mushrooms on public land. In certain regions, the number of mushrooms that may be picked may be limited, and some species may be off-limits altogether due to protection laws.

Practice Responsible Foraging

It is crucial to use sustainable gathering procedures in order to safeguard the health of the ecosystem and guarantee that future generations will have the opportunity to enjoy mushroom foraging. The following are some suggestions for responsible foraging:

- You should try to avoid choosing young or immature mushrooms since they haven't had the opportunity to multiply and release their spores yet.
- Be careful not to overharvest in a single spot. It is important for the population of fungi that you preserve some of the mushrooms so that they may continue to develop and reproduce.
- Cutting the stem of the mushroom with a forage knife or scissors is preferable to yanking it out of the ground, which might cause harm to the mycelium because of its sensitive nature.

- Carry the mushrooms in a mesh bag or a basket to enable the spores to spread while you walk, which will help the mushrooms thrive in the future.

Be Ready for Anything and Keep Yourself Safe

When going mushroom hunting, it is really necessary to have all of your equipment ready and put a high priority on being safe. The following are some suggestions for hunting mushrooms safely:

- If you want to identify mushrooms, bring a field guide with you or use a trustworthy app on your mobile device.
- Put on some proper gear, such as long trousers, some shoes that aren't going to fall apart, and a cap, in order to protect oneself from sun exposure and insects like ticks.
- When going on a hunt in the woods, it is a good idea to have a compass or a GPS device with you since it is easy to get lost.
- In the event of a medical emergency, you should always have a first aid kit with you and be informed of the location of the closest medical institution.

Methods for the Conservation and Stockpiling of Mushrooms

It is crucial to know how to properly store and preserve mushrooms in order to keep their taste and nutritional value intact once you have successfully collected them via foraging.

Housekeeping

To remove dirt and debris from the mushrooms, gently clean them by brushing them with a soft brush or wiping them down with a moist cloth. It is best to avoid soaking mushrooms in water since doing so will cause them to absorb moisture and become mushy.

Methods for the Storage of Fresh Mushrooms

Fresh mushrooms should be kept in the refrigerator in a paper bag or a moist towel that is wrapped around them. This ensures that the mushrooms do not get slimy and enables air circulation to reach all of them. The majority of mushroom varieties may be kept in this manner for up to a week.

Drying

Drying mushrooms is an effective method for preserving them for an extended period of time. Cut the mushrooms into uniformly thin slices, then spread them out on a drying rack or screen in a location that has plenty of ventilation. There is also the option of using a food dehydrator or an oven with the door cracked slightly and set to the lowest temperature possible. You may keep dried mushrooms for up to a year in a dark, cold area if you store them in an airtight container.

Freezing

One further way to preserve mushrooms is to put them in the freezer; this works especially well for species that do not dry out well, such as chanterelles. To prepare mushrooms for freezing, first, wash and then slice them. The next step is to brown the mushrooms and release their liquid by sautéing them in a little butter or oil until they reach the desired level of browning. After allowing the mushrooms to cool, place them in a container that can be frozen before proceeding to store them in the freezer for up to six months.

The Medicinal Properties of Mushrooms

Mushrooms have been prized for their culinary applications as well as their potential therapeutic benefits for a very long time. Compounds with immune-enhancing, anti-cancer, and anti-inflammatory properties have been found in some species.

Ganoderma lucidum (Reishi)

It is well known that reishi mushrooms have qualities that modulate the immune system and fight cancer. Triterpenes, which are found in them, are molecules that have been shown to help decrease inflammation and limit the development of tumors.

Lentinula edodes (shiitake)

A substance known as lentinan may be found in shiitake mushrooms. This substance has been the subject of research because of its potential to strengthen the immune system and suppress the formation of tumors. In addition to being rich in necessary minerals and vitamins, shiitake mushrooms are also a strong source of vitamins B and D.

Grifola frondosa (Maitake)

The immune-boosting and cancer-fighting properties of maitake mushrooms have been the subject of much research. They include a polysaccharide known as beta-glucan, which has the potential to boost the immune system and assist in the battle against cancer cells.

Hericium erinaceus, "Lion's Mane."

The possible neuroprotective and cognitive-enhancing effects of lion's mane mushrooms are well established. Hericenones and erinacines, two of the molecules that they include, are thought to increase the generation of nerve growth factors and maintain the health of the brain.

Turkey Tail (Trametes versicolor)

Researchers have examined turkey tail mushrooms for their potential to strengthen the immune system and fight cancer. They include polysaccharide peptide (PSP) and polysaccharide-K (PSK), both of which have been demonstrated to promote immune function and suppress tumor development in research studies.

Benefits of Consuming Medicinal Mushrooms as Part of Your Diet

Consuming medicinal mushrooms as whole foods, incorporating them into culinary preparations, or using them as dietary supplements in the form of powders, capsules, or extracts are all viable options. When adding medicinal mushrooms to your diet, it is crucial to acquire high-quality items and speak with a healthcare practitioner to establish the optimum dose and confirm that there are no contraindications with any of the drugs you are currently taking or health concerns you have.

The Importance of Mycology in Today's Scientific Community

In recent years, mycology, which is the study of fungi, has garnered significant prominence for its potential uses in a variety of scientific sectors, including medicine, agriculture, and the repair of polluted environments, among others.

Research in the Field of Medicine

Fungi are responsible for the production of a diverse array of bioactive chemicals, many of which have potential use in the medical field. The fungus Penicillium chrysogenum invented one of the most significant antibiotics, penicillin. Penicillin is one of the most extensively used antibiotics. There is research going on to see if other fungi-produced substances have the potential to treat diseases like cancer, Alzheimer's disease, and Parkinson's disease.

Agriculture and Pest Control

Through the processes of decomposition and mycorrhizal association, fungi are an essential component in keeping soil healthy and fostering the development of plants. Mycologists are also investigating the possibility of utilizing fungi as biocontrol agents, which would include using them to combat illnesses and pests that endanger agricultural production.

Environmental Cleanup and Restoration Work

Because of their remarkable capacity to degrade a broad variety of organic and inorganic chemicals, fungi are becoming increasingly important components in the process of environmental restoration. Researchers are looking at the possibility of using fungus to clean up polluted soil, water, and air, as well as to degrade waste plastics.

Mushroom growing provides newcomers with a plethora of choices, from the enjoyment of delectable gourmet mushrooms cultivated at home to the investigation of the fascinating world of fungus and the ecological, gastronomic, and medicinal aspects of various species. You will be able to go on a wonderful trip into the world of mycology after you have a grasp of the many varieties of mushrooms, their methods of identification, and the best procedures for gathering, storing, and preserving mushrooms. You will be more prepared to safely and sustainably enjoy the numerous advantages of mushrooms as your knowledge and experience increase while also contributing to a deeper understanding and appreciation of these extraordinary creatures. This is because you will have contributed to a greater appreciation of their unique qualities.

Chapter 2: Different Substrates for Mushroom Cultivation

It is crucial that you understand what a substrate is and why it is necessary before we begin discussing the numerous substrates that may be used for the growing of mushrooms. The substance that mushrooms grow on in order to receive their nutrition is referred to as a substrate. The proper substrate will provide the mycelium and fruiting bodies of mushrooms with the nutrients, water, and structure required for their continued expansion and development. In this chapter, we will talk about the many kinds of substrates that are appropriate for mushroom culture, as well as the unique needs that each of those substrates has in terms of humidity, temperature, and light.

Common Substrates for Mushroom Cultivation

Mushrooms may be grown on a broad range of substrates, each of which comes with its own set of benefits and drawbacks when utilized for growth purposes. The following are some of the substrates that are used most frequently:

Straw

For the cultivation of a wide variety of mushroom species, notably oyster mushrooms (Pleurotus spp.), straw is a preferred choice of substrate. It is a low-cost and readily accessible substance that functions as an ideal framework for the development of mycelial strands. To produce a growth media that is richer in nutrients, you may either use straw by itself or combine it with other substrates.

Sawdust

Sawdust is another kind of substrate that is often used in the growing of mushrooms. It is especially well-suited for wood-loving mushrooms like shiitake (Lentinula edodes) and lion's mane (Hericium erinaceus), such as oyster mushrooms (Pleurotus ostreatus). Because softwood sawdust may include substances that prevent the development of mushrooms, it is recommended that the sawdust be derived from hardwoods such as oak. In order to produce a product that is more nutrient-dense, sawdust is often combined with other components, such as wheat bran or soybean hulls.

Wood Logs

Mushrooms may be grown on wood logs, which serve as a natural substrate for the process. This is especially true for mushroom varieties that flourish well in a forest setting, such as shiitake and maitake (Grifola frondosa). Logs made of hardwoods, such as oak, maple, or beech, are excellent for the growing of mushrooms. It is important that the logs have recently been cut and show no symptoms of rotting or other forms of fungus development.

Compost

For the cultivation of a wide range of mushrooms, including Agaricus bisporus (white button mushrooms) and Agaricus subrufescens (almond portobello), compost, and more specifically compost made from mushrooms or horse dung, is an ideal substrate. The compost needs to have a good amount of age on it and should not include any dangerous chemicals or pesticides.

Grain

In the first stage of mushroom development, which is referred to as spawn production, grain substrates like rye, wheat, or millet are often used as growing mediums. The grain offers a nutrient-dense environment for the development of mycelium and may be readily combined with other substrates to produce a growing media that is ideal for fruiting.

Preparing Substrates for Mushroom Cultivation

It is very necessary to properly prepare the substrates in order to successfully cultivate mushrooms. The following procedures are frequently included during the process:

Hydration

In order to provide the mycelial development with the required amount of moisture, the substrate has to be hydrated. The optimal moisture content varies based on the substrate and the kind of mushroom being grown, but it's often anywhere between 55 and 75 percent of the total. The substrate should have a moist, but not wet, feel to it, and when pressed, it should not release any water.

Sterilization or Pasteurization

Prior to being inoculated with mushroom mycelium, the substrate has to be either sterilized or pasteurized so that it does not get contaminated with unwelcome microbes. Pasteurization utilizes temperatures between 160- and 180degrees Fahrenheit (71 and 82 degrees Celsius) for a longer length of time (1-2 hours), while sterilization utilizes higher temperatures (typically 250 degrees Fahrenheit or 121 degrees Celsius) for a shorterperiod of time (1-2 hours). The substrate and the particular species of mushroom that are being farmed are factors that should be considered while deciding between sterilization and pasteurization. Some species, like the Agaricus bisporus, can only grow on substrates that have been sterilized, whilst others, like the oyster mushroom, can grow on substrates that have been pasteurized.

The Process of Inoculation and Cooling

In order to inoculate the substrate with mushroom spawn after it has been sterilized or pasteurized, the substrate must first be cooled down to a suitable temperature. Temperatures in the appropriate range for growing a particular species of mushroom should be maintained, which is often in the range of 21 to 27 degrees Celsius (70 to 80 degrees Fahrenheit). After the substrate has had time to cool, it may be infected with mushroom spawn in one of two ways: either the spawn can be mixed directly into the substrate, or the spawn can be layered on top of the substrate in a container.

Humidity, Temperature, and Light Requirements for Mushroom Growth

To achieve their full potential in terms of growth and development, mushrooms must fulfill certain environmental criteria. These needs include a certain level of humidity, temperature, and light, the precise levels of which change according to the kind of mushroom.

Humidity

Because it influences both the growth of the mycelium and the creation of the fruiting bodies, humidity is an extremely important factor in mushroom development. The ideal relative humidity for the vast majority of mushroom species is somewhere in the range of 80-95%. Utilizing a humidifier, sprinkling the substrate, or covering the growing container with a plastic sheet or top to preserve moisture are all viable options for maintaining humidity in the environment in which plants are being grown.

Temperature

The optimal growing temperature for a given species of mushroom might vary greatly from one to the next. Some mushrooms, such as white button and shiitake, grow best at temperatures between 55- and 65 degrees Fahrenheit (12 and 18 degrees Celsius), while others, such as oyster mushrooms, do best in temperatures between 65- and 75 degrees Fahrenheit (18 and 24 degrees Celsius). In order to provide the best possible circumstances for mycelial development and fruiting, the temperature of the growing environment should be carefully maintained and monitored.

Light

Although photosynthesis in mushrooms is not dependent on light like it is in plants, light is nevertheless important for the growth and development of mushroom-fruiting bodies. Some kinds of mushrooms, such as Agaricus bisporus, only need to be exposed to a little amount of light, while others, such as shiitake and oyster mushrooms, thrive when they are exposed to indirect or diffused light. It is important to do a study to determine the ideal lighting conditions for each species of mushroom and then replicate those circumstances in the growing habitat.

Mushroom Cultivation Techniques

Mushrooms may be grown using a variety of different methods, each of which has both benefits and difficulties associated with it. The following are some of the most often-used methods:

The Method of Using a Bag

On straw or sawdust substrates, one of the most common methods for cultivating mushrooms, notably oyster mushrooms, is to use a bag method. First, the substrate is hydrated; next, it is either pasteurized or sterilized; and last, the mushroom spawn is added. After that, the infected substrate is placed within a specific filter bag, which enables an exchange of air but maintains a level of protection against contamination. After being sealed, the bag is then placed in an environment that is conducive to growing mushrooms so that the mycelium may colonize the substrate. After the colonization process is over, the bag is either opened completely, or it is punctured with many holes so that the mushrooms may produce fruit.

The Method of Using a Tray or Tub

Growing mushrooms in shallow containers, such as plastic trays or storage tubs, is what's involved in the tray or tub technique of cultivation. After the substrate has been prepared and infected with mushroom spawn, it is put in the containers, which then have a plastic sheet or lid placed on top of them to maintain the appropriate level of humidity. This technique is often used for the cultivation of Agaricus bisporus and other species that call for a casing layer, which is put to the surface of the substrate after colonization has taken place.

The Method of the Bottle

Growing mushrooms on sawdust or grain substrates using the bottle method is a method that makes effective use of available space. Before the substrate is packed into bottles made of glass or plastic, it must first undergo preparation, then sterilization, and finally inoculation with mushroom spawn. After that, the bottles are put into an environment that has their temperature and humidity carefully managed so that the mycelium may colonize it. After the colonization process is over, the bottles are put into an environment with the right amount of light to start the fruiting process. The cultivation of shiitake and oyster mushrooms often makes use of this particular technology.

Application of the Log Method

The log technique of growing mushrooms is a more natural way of growing mushrooms that imitates the circumstances that are present in an environment that is wooded. Either by drilling holes in freshly cut hardwood logs and inserting spawn plugs shaped like dowels or by distributing sawdust spawn over the log's surface and sealing it with wax, fresh hardwood logs are infected with mushroom spawn to encourage the growth of mushrooms. After the logs have been infected, they are moved to a shaded and wet environment and left there for the mycelium to colonize the wood. This process may take anything from a few months to more than a year to complete, depending on the kind of mushroom and the size of the wood. After the first phase of colonization has been over, the logs may be submerged in water to encourage fruiting.

The Method of Using an Outdoor Bed

Mushrooms are grown using the outdoor bed technique in a prepared outside space, such as a garden bed or a plot of ground specifically designated for mushroom cultivation. After excavating a shallow trench and filling it with the proper substrate, the area is prepared for the cultivation of mushrooms by having the trench infected with mushroom spawn. In order to prevent the substrate from drying up and to create an environment that is conducive to the development of mycelium, it is covered with a layer of dirt or mulch after it has been infected. The cultivation of wine cap mushrooms (Stropharia rugosoannulata) and other species that perform well in natural settings is often accomplished via the use of this technique.

Factors to Consider When Choosing a Mushroom Cultivation Technique

When choosing a method of growing mushrooms, there are a few things that need to be taken into consideration, including the following:

Mushroom Species

The culture method that is used will be determined to some extent by the specific substrate and environmental requirements imposed by each mushroom species. For instance, oyster mushrooms may be readily produced using the bag or bottle technique, but shiitake mushrooms are often grown on logs or sawdust blocks. Both of these methods can be found in mushroom cultivation.

Available Space

The selection of the growth method will also be influenced by the quantity of space at one's disposal for growing mushrooms. Others, such as the log or outdoor bed approach, take more area and may be more suited for larger-scale production, while others, like the bottle method, are space-efficient and appropriate for small-scale home cultivation. Some methods, such as the bottle method, are suitable for small-scale home growing.

Financial Plan and Available Means

When deciding the method of mushroom production to use, it is important to take into account both the price and accessibility of various resources, such as substrates, spawns, and equipment. Some techniques, such as the bag method, involve the use of specialized filter bags as well as a setup for either pasteurization or sterilization. Other methods, such as the log method, depend solely on natural materials and need very little in the way of technology.

Experience Level

It is important, especially for those who are just starting out, to take into consideration the amount of difficulty and expertise necessary for the various ways of mushroom growth. Some ways, such as the tray or tub approach, are basic and suitable for beginners, whilst other methods, such as the bottle or log method, may call for more knowledge and ability.

Advanced Techniques and Tips for Mushroom Cultivation

This part digs into more sophisticated strategies and recommendations that may assist you in making the most of your efforts to cultivate mushrooms, in contrast to the preceding section, which concentrated on the fundamentals of mushroom cultivation. These techniques may help you raise your production, enhance the quality of your mushrooms, and fix problems that may occur while you are growing them.

Optimizing Substrate Composition

As was noted before, the substrate is an essential component in the culture of mushrooms since it supplies the mycelial growth and fruiting with the nutrients, water, and structure they need to flourish. You may improve the development of your mushrooms and the yield you get from them by learning the unique nutritional needs of the type of mushroom you are growing and by fine-tuning the composition of the substrate you use.

Nitrogen Content

The amount of nitrogen that is present in the substrate is an important factor in the growth and development of mushroom colonies. Nitrogen is necessary for the metabolic activities that take place in the mushroom mycelium since it is a key component of proteins as well as other vital cellular components. The nitrogen needs of various mushroom species may be accommodated by making adjustments to the chemical make-up of the substrate. To boost the amount of nitrogen present in the substrate, components like wheat bran, soybean hulls, or cottonseed meal may be used in the mix. However, care should be taken not to exceed the ideal amounts of nitrogen since doing so might lead to excessive production of ammonia and hinder the development of mushrooms.

The Relationship Between Carbon and Nitrogen

When attempting to optimize the substrate composition for mushroom culture, one of the most important factors to take into consideration is the carbon-to-nitrogen (C: N) ratio. For mycelial development to occur, there must be a healthy balance between the sources of energy (carbon) and the building blocks (nitrogen). This may be achieved by maintaining an acceptable C:N ratio. The optimal ratio of carbon to nitrogen in mushroom cultivation varies from species to species of the fungi being grown. For instance, oyster mushrooms thrive best in an environment with a carbon-to-nitrogen ratio of around 15:1 to 20:1, but shiitake mushrooms like a carbon-to-nitrogen ratio of 30:1 to 50:1. Modifying the quantities of the various substrate components or adding supplements that are rich in carbon or nitrogen are both viable options for achieving the desired C:N ratio adjustment.

Mineral Content

Phosphorus, potassium, calcium, and magnesium are some of the minerals that mushrooms need in order to achieve their full potential as a crop. Even though the majority of substrates already contain appropriate levels of these minerals, the use of mineral supplements like gypsum or rock phosphate may assist in improving the overall nutritional quality of the substrate and boost the development of mushrooms.

Enhancing the Existing Conditions of the Environment

To ensure that mycelial development and mushroom production are maximized to their full potential, it is essential to optimize environmental parameters, including humidity, temperature, and light. These conditions may be maintained and monitored more precisely and consistently with the use of advanced procedures and technology, which can lead to improvements in the outcomes.

Automated Control of the Relative Humidity

Automated humidity management systems make use of sensors and other pieces of machinery, such as humidifiers and dehumidifiers, to maintain the ideal amount of humidity in the growing environment. This helps to ensure that the plant is able to reach its full potential. These devices have the potential to assist in guaranteeing regular humidity levels throughout the growing process, therefore lowering the danger of contamination and encouraging the development of healthy mushrooms.

Temperature Control

It is crucial to keep temperatures stable and at appropriate levels during the whole growing phase of mushrooms if one wants to achieve maximum yield and quality. The use of sophisticated temperature control systems, such as heaters or air conditioning units with thermostatic controls, may assist in preserving the temperature that is optimal for the particular species of mushroom that you are cultivating. In addition, monitoring tools such as digital thermometers and data loggers may assist in tracking temperature changes and ensuring that the growth environment stays within the appropriate range. This helps to guarantee that the plant is able to reach its full potential.

The Regulation of the Light

As was just said, the presence of light in an environment is important to the development and maturation of mushroom-fruiting bodies. You may stimulate fruiting that is more robust and consistent if you optimize the light conditions for the particular type of mushroom that you are growing. Innovative lighting solutions, such as LED grow lights or adjustable light timers, may assist in providing your mushrooms with the ideal light intensity, light duration, and light spectrum for their growth. These technologies have the potential to assist in energy conservation as well as lower the total cost of mushroom growth.

Advanced Cultivation Techniques

There are a number of modern growing methods that, when combined with the optimization of the substrate composition and ambient conditions, may assist in boosting the quantity as well as the quality of the mushrooms you grow.

Liquid Culture Inoculation

In liquid culture inoculation, rather than cultivating mushroom mycelium on a solid substrate like grain or agar, the mycelium is grown in a liquid nutrient solution. This form of growth is known as "liquid culture inoculation." Because liquid culture inoculation allows for the creation of a greater volume of mycelial biomass in a shorter amount of time and with greater efficiency, it speeds up the colonization process and results in enhanced mushroom output. It is possible to inoculate a liquid culture by using a sterilized liquid nutrient solution, such as potato dextrose broth or malt extract, and then adding a tiny quantity of mushroom mycelium or spores to the inoculated solution. This process is known as liquid culture inoculation.

Cloning Wild Mushrooms

The process of cloning wild mushrooms involves capturing the genetic material of a wild mushroom specimen in order to develop the specimen in an environment that is under stricter control. You are able to keep the wild mushroom's distinctive taste, texture, and look by cloning it, which also gives you the opportunity to possibly increase the genetic variety of your cultured mushroom stock. Cloning may be accomplished by removing a tiny piece of sterile tissue from the inside of the fruiting body of a wild mushroom and placing it on a sterile agar medium for mycelial development. This is the first step in the cloning process.

Environmental Manipulation

The term "environmental manipulation" refers to the process of altering the circumstances of the environment in which the mushrooms are grown in order to stimulate the development of certain phases or traits in the mushrooms. You could, for instance, be able to induce the creation of bigger, more robust fruiting bodies in the plant by decreasing the temperature of the growth environment or raising the quantities of carbon dioxide in the atmosphere. In a similar vein, if you modify the light spectrum or intensity, you may be able to improve the color, texture, or other aspects of the mushrooms' appearance that are aesthetically pleasing. Experimenting with the management of the environment may help you fine-tune the growth and development of your mushrooms, resulting in a product that is more to your liking after it has been harvested.

Common Solutions to Problems Encountered in Mushroom Cultivation

During the process of cultivating mushrooms, problems might appear even with meticulous planning and carrying out of the steps. The following are some prevalent issues, as well as possible remedies for them:

Suppress the Growth of the Mycelium

There are a number of potential reasons for slow mycelial development, including a lack of enough nourishment, an incorrect environment in terms of temperature or humidity, or contamination. In order to fix this problem, you will need to make sure that the nutritional needs of the mushroom species you are cultivating are met by the composition of your substrate and that the ambient conditions are within the appropriate range. In addition, check for any evidence of contamination, such as off-odors, discoloration, or competing fungal or bacterial growth. If you find any of these, throw out the item.

Poor Fruiting or Low Yields

Inadequate environmental conditions, such as a lack of light, low humidity, or unsuitable temperature, may lead to poor fruiting or low yields. These circumstances can also negatively affect the quality of the fruit. Make sure that your growing environment satisfies the particular conditions that are necessary for the cultivation of your mushroom species in order to achieve better fruiting and yield. In addition, if you want your mushrooms to grow and develop to their full potential, you should investigate the possibility of conducting experiments with various combinations of substrates and methods of culture.

Contamination

In the production of mushrooms, contamination is a frequent problem that may result in decreased yields, mushrooms of low quality, or even the full collapse of the crop. When preparing substrates and equipment, as well as maintaining a clean and regulated growth environment, you should apply correct sterilization and hygiene practices. This will help reduce the likelihood that you will introduce contamination. In the case that contamination does take place, it is vital to locate the source of the problem, remove any impacted goods, and take measures to avoid such incidents in the future.

Cultivating mushrooms may be an interesting and satisfying pastime or business enterprise since it provides a continuous supply of mushrooms that are not only tasty but also healthy and useful for medical purposes. Beginners may successfully start on a trip into the world of mycology by first gaining an awareness of the many substrates that can be used for mushroom production, the precise needs for humidity, temperature, and light, as well as the numerous cultivation methods that are accessible. You may boost the quantity, quality, and consistency of your mushrooms by making use of more modern methods and by making your mushroom cultivating process as efficient as possible. You may improve your mushroom cultivation abilities and take advantage of the numerous advantages that come with producing these wonderful and adaptable creatures if you put in the effort and continue to educate yourself.

Chapter 3: Pasteurization and Inoculation in Mushroom Cultivation

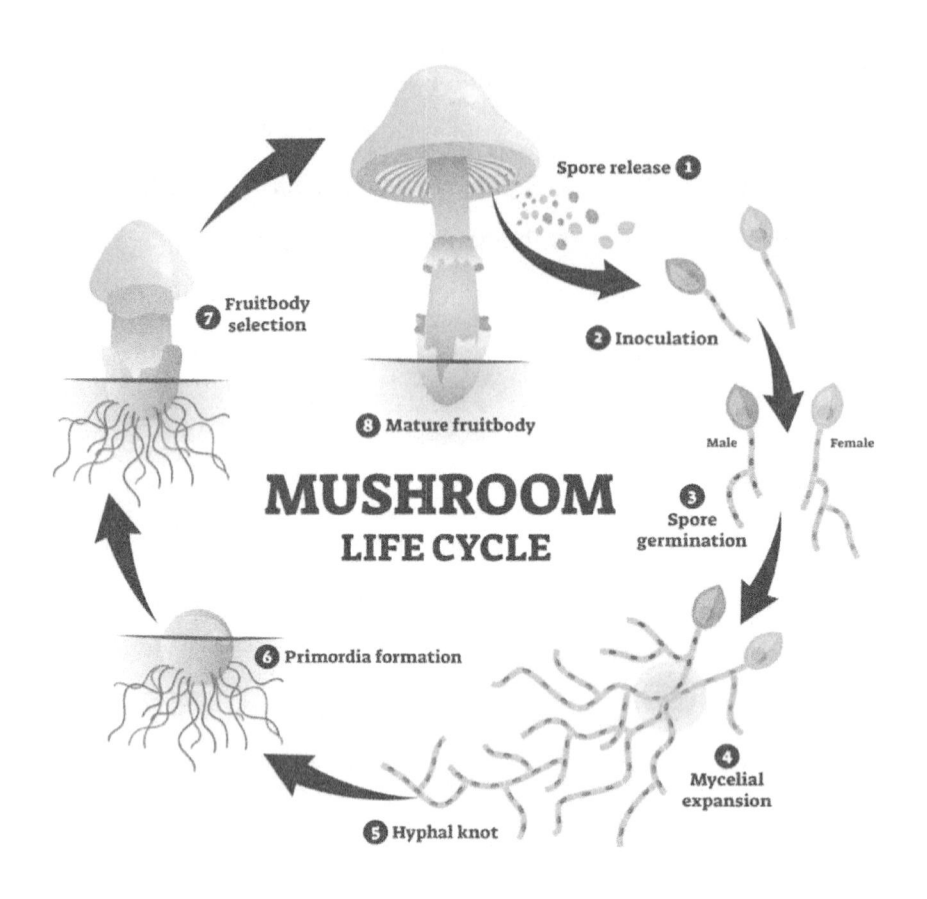

In the next chapter, we will delve into the vital steps of mushroom culture that are known as pasteurization and inoculation procedures. These two procedures play an essential part in guaranteeing the healthy growth and development of your mushrooms while simultaneously lowering the likelihood that they will get contaminated. In this lesson, you will learn about the many techniques that are used for pasteurization and inoculation, as well as the advantages and disadvantages of each approach.

Pasteurization in Mushroom Cultivation

Before the mushroom mycelium is introduced to the substrate, a procedure called pasteurization is performed in order to minimize the amount of potentially dangerous microorganisms that are already present in the substrate. These microorganisms include bacteria and mold spores. This method is essential to the production of mushrooms because it provides an environment that is more conducive to the growth and development of the species of mushroom that is wanted while simultaneously reducing the likelihood that the environment will get contaminated by organisms that are vying for the same resources.

Common Pasteurization Methods

There are a few different ways of pasteurization that are employed in the growing of mushrooms, and each one has both benefits and drawbacks. The choice of approach is determined by a number of criteria, including the nature of the substrate that is being used, the scope of your operation, and the resources that are at your disposal.

Hot Water Immersion

Immersion in hot water is one of the ways of pasteurization that is most often used in the process of growing mushrooms on a small scale. During this procedure, the substrate is kept immersed in water that is heated to a specified temperature for a predetermined amount of time, which is normally between one and two hours and ranges from 70 to 85 degrees Celsius. The heat eliminates many of the undesirable bacteria that are present in the substrate while yet maintaining the helpful microbes that are essential for the development of the mycelium.

Advantages:

- Simple and efficient in terms of cost
- Appropriate for use in less extensive settings
- Suitable for use with a variety of substrates

Disadvantages:

- Less precise temperature regulation
- The possibility is that the substrate may become too moist.
- Requiring a significant amount of energy on a wider scale

Steam Pasteurization

In steam pasteurization, the substrate is heated to a specified temperature, which is typically in the range of 70 to 85 degrees Celsius (about 160 degrees Fahrenheit), using steam as the heat source. This technique is often used in mushroom culture operations that are conducted on a bigger scale and is capable of being carried out in specialist apparatus such as steam chambers or autoclaves.

Advantages:
- Precise temperature control
- Better moisture control
- Adaptable to accommodate large-scale activities

Disadvantages:
- More sophisticated setup and equipment needed
- The costs of the first investment are higher.
- Energy-intensive

Pasteurization Via Chemical Process

In the process of chemical pasteurization, unwelcome microorganisms in the substrate are eliminated by the use of chemical agents like lime or hydrogen peroxide, for example. In this approach, the substrate is treated with a chemical solution, which, while it does not need the use of heat, is very successful in lowering the number of hazardous bacteria present.

Advantages:
- Because there is no need for heat, the amount of energy used is decreased.
- Suitable for use with substrates that are heat sensitive
- It can need less manual effort than some of the other approaches

Disadvantages:
- The possibility that the substrate contains chemical residues
- It could be less effective than techniques that include heat
- It is important to use caution while working with certain compounds.

Inoculation in Mushroom Cultivation

Inoculation is the technique of inserting mycelium or spores of a fungus onto a prepared substrate in order to start the growth and colonization process. In order to successfully cultivate mushrooms, it is necessary to complete this phase because it enables the chosen species of mushroom to establish itself inside the substrate and begin the process of generating fruiting bodies.

Popular Inoculation Methods

Mushroom farming makes use of a variety of different inoculation techniques, each of which has both advantages and disadvantages. The kind of mushroom species that are being grown, the substrate that is being utilized, and the volume of your operation are all important considerations that should be taken into account when selecting a cultivation technique.

Inoculation of Grain and Sprouts

Inoculating different substrates with grain spawn is a common practice these days. Some examples of such substrates are straw, wood chips, and sawdust. In this technique, grain spawn is produced by first cultivating mushroom mycelium on a sterile grain like rye, wheat, or millet. Other grains that may be used include millet. After this step, the grain spawn is combined with the prepared substrate, which makes it possible for the mycelium to colonize and spread throughout the new substance.

Advantages:
- Adaptable and suitable for use with a wide range of substrates
- Effective for a wide variety of types of mushrooms
- Simple to manipulate and incorporate into the substrate.

Disadvantages:
- Sterilization of the grain must be performed before use; there is a risk of contamination during handling and mixing.
- Large-scale activities could need the purchase of more resources or equipment.

Liquid Culture Inoculation

The development of mushroom mycelium is accomplished by a process known as liquid culture inoculation. This process takes place in a liquid nutrient solution, such as potato dextrose broth or malt extract. Once the mycelium has developed and established a thick network in the liquid, the culture is either injected directly into the substrate using a syringe or combined with the substrate in a sterile environment. This is done once the mycelium has completed its growth and formation in the liquid. Through the use of this technique, fast colonization and expansion of the mycelium throughout the substrate are made possible.

Advantages:

- Quicker timeframes for colonization in comparison to previous approaches.
- Reduced potential for contamination during the inoculation process
- Easily scalable to accommodate more extensive operations

Disadvantages:

- Requires sterile equipment and a clean atmosphere for preparation
- It can be more difficult to master for those just starting out.
- It's possible that some types of mushrooms won't react well to liquid culture inoculation.

The Inoculation of Spores

In the technique of spore inoculation, mushroom spores are introduced directly into the substrate in order to commence the development and colonization of the mushroom. This technique may be carried out either by sprinkling dry spore powder over the substrate or by using a spore syringe to apply the spores directly to the surface. Although spore inoculation is not often utilized in the production of commercial mushrooms, it is a method that may be helpful for individuals who grow mushrooms as a hobby or who are interested in doing research on wild mushroom strains.

Advantages:

- It can be used for the cultivation of many kinds of wild mushrooms
- Appropriate for use in limited-scale activities or for experimenting.
- The method is simple to use and not too expensive for novices

Disadvantages:

- The colonization process takes longer compared to other approaches.
- There is a greater potential for contamination during the inoculation process.
- Some mushroom species may be difficult to cultivate from spores.

Monitoring and Optimizing the Growth Environment

It is vital to maintain and optimize the growing environment throughout the whole mushroom cultivation process in order to guarantee the production of successful mushrooms. This part will address the elements that impact mushroom development, such as temperature, humidity, light, and air exchange, as well as how to monitor and alter these conditions to create the most conducive habitat for your selected mushroom species. Temperature, humidity, light, and air exchange are just some of the aspects that will be discussed.

Temperature

In order to achieve optimum growth and development, the mycelium and fruiting bodies of mushrooms have temperature needs that must be met. Because these needs might change from species to species, it is essential to do a study and have a solid understanding of the temperature range that is optimum for the sort of mushroom you are trying to grow.

Keeping an Eye on the Temperature

Obtaining an accurate reading of the temperature in your growing environment requires the use of a dependable digital thermometer or a temperature and humidity monitor. Investing in one of these devices is the first step toward achieving this goal. Place the monitor in the growing area, making sure that it is not directly exposed to any sources of heat or sunshine since this might cause the results to be erroneous.

Adjusting Temperature

If the temperature in your growing environment is either too high or too low, you will probably need to make some modifications in order to get it within the ideal range for the kind of mushroom you are cultivating. The following are some ways that may be used to adjust the temperature:

- Putting in or taking out items that serve as insulation
- Changing the settings on the heating or cooling apparatus
- Controlling the flow of air and the ventilation
- Changing the location of your growth area or the configuration of it

Humidity

Because it helps to keep the moisture content of the substrate at a consistent level and makes it possible for normal metabolic activities to take place, humidity plays an important part in the growth and development of mushrooms. Because the humidity needs of various mushroom species may range widely, it is essential to do enough study and get a solid understanding of the appropriate humidity levels for the species you want to cultivate.

Keeping an eye on the humidity

Obtaining an accurate reading of the humidity level in your growing environment requires the use of a dependable digital hygrometer or a monitor that measures both temperature and humidity. Position the monitor in the growing area, taking care that it is not directly exposed to any water or other sources of moisture since this might cause the readings to be erroneous.

Adjusting Humidity

If the humidity in your growing environment is either too high or too low, you will probably need to make some modifications in order to get it within the ideal range for the kind of mushroom you are cultivating. The following are some strategies that may be used to manage humidity:

- Using humidifiers or dehumidifiers
- Modifying the flow of air and the ventilation
- The incorporation of elements into the substrate that is capable of storing moisture, such as coco coir or peat moss
- In the event that it is required, spray the growing area with water.

Light

Even though mushrooms do not get their energy from photosynthesis as plants do, they nevertheless need to be exposed to some amount of light in order for their fruiting bodies to grow properly. Because the precise light needs of each species of mushroom might vary, it is vital to do a study and have an understanding of the perfect light conditions for the species you have selected to cultivate.

Light for Keeping Watch

Consider using a light meter or a monitor that measures temperature, humidity, and light all in one unit in order to keep track of the amount of light that is present in your growing environment. Place the monitor in the growth area while taking precautions to prevent it from being directly illuminated by natural or artificial light sources since this might cause the readings to be erroneous.

Modifying the Lighting

It's possible that you'll need to make some alterations to your growing environment if the light exposure there isn't ideal for the kind of mushrooms you're cultivating. The following are some strategies that may be used to adjust the amount of light:

- Utilizing man-made sources of illumination, such as LED or fluorescent lighting
- Modifying the length of time as well as the amount of light exposure
- Changing the location of your growing space or the arrangement of it to get the most out of the natural light

Air Exchange

It is very necessary to have enough air circulation in order to have a healthy growth environment for mushrooms. Fresh air supplies the oxygen that is required for mycelial respiration, and it also helps to avoid the accumulation of carbon dioxide and other byproducts of metabolic waste. Additionally, regular air exchange helps to manage temperature and humidity levels, which in turn decreases the danger of contamination from mold and other undesirable organisms.

Monitoring Air Exchange

You may use carbon dioxide (CO_2) monitors or air quality monitors to keep an eye on the air exchange in your growing environment. These monitors assess a variety of factors, including the amounts of CO_2 in the air, as well as temperature and humidity. Place the monitor in the growing area, taking care not to position it so that it is directly exposed to any sources of airflow or ventilation, as this might cause the results to be erroneous.

Adjusting Air Exchange

It's possible that you'll need to make some alterations to your growing environment if the air exchange there isn't ideal for the kind of mushrooms you're cultivating. The following are some ways that may be used to manage air exchange:

- Installing and modifying fans or ventilation systems
- Adjusting the amount of airflow by opening and shutting windows and vents
- Increasing the number of air-cleaning plants or installing air filters in order to better the air quality
- Making adjustments to the structure or configuration of your growing space so as to maximize the flow of natural air

Common Solutions to Problems Encountered in Mushroom Cultivation

Mushroom growing, like any other kind of agricultural effort, may come with its fair share of difficulties and problems. In this part of the guide, we'll go over some of the more typical problems that crop up throughout the cultivation process, as well as give some troubleshooting advice and solutions to help you get over these obstacles.

Contamination

In mushroom production, contamination is a frequent problem because undesired microorganisms, such as mold and bacteria, may compete with the mushroom mycelium for nutrients and hamper development. Mold and bacteria are two examples of undesirable microorganisms. In order to reduce the likelihood of contamination:

- Maintain high standards of cleanliness and hygiene in the growing space you have.
- Make use of substrates and instruments that have been pasteurized or sterilized.
- Keep an eye on everything and make sure the atmosphere is in good shape.
- To stop the virulence of dangerous pathogens from spreading, contaminated substrates or cultures should be isolated.

Mycelial Growth That Is Sluggish or Completely Stopped

Consider the following criteria in the event that you find that the mycelial development in your substrate is either sluggish or has come to a standstill:

- Make sure that the substrate has been sufficiently pasteurized or sterilized in order to get rid of any bacteria that may compete with you.
- Make any necessary modifications to the temperature and humidity levels in your growth environment once you have checked them.
- Examine your technique of inoculation and make certain that the mycelium or spores you are utilizing are in good condition and able to reproduce.
- You should think about the age of your substrate materials as well as their quality since older substrates that are nutrient-depleted may not support ideal development.

Poor Fruiting or Yield

Take into consideration the following possibilities if you find that your mushrooms are not fruiting properly or generating a poor yield:

- Check to ensure that you are giving the correct amount of light exposure for the kind of mushrooms you are cultivating.
- Your growth environment should include temperature, humidity, and air exchange levels that are monitored and maintained at ideal levels.
- Make sure that your substrate has a suitable amount of nutrients to enable the growth of fruiting bodies.
- To encourage fruiting in your mushrooms, you may want to think about employing a casing layer if one is available for that particular species.

Mushroom Development That Is Abnormal or Malformed

A number of different things, including environmental stress, pollution, or genetic anomalies, may lead to the formation of mushrooms that are misshapen or otherwise aberrant. In order to solve this problem:

- Check the ambient parameters, such as temperature, humidity, and light, and make any necessary adjustments to get them within the ideal range for the variety of mushrooms you are cultivating.
- Conduct a thorough inspection of your growing space for any indications of microbial contamination or insect infestation, and take remedial action as required.
- It is possible that certain strains of mushrooms are more prone to aberrant growth than others. If this is the case, you may want to try using a different strain or species of mushroom.

The processes of pasteurization and inoculation are essential phases in the culture of mushrooms. These techniques ensure the healthy growth and development of the species of mushroom you want to cultivate while reducing the likelihood that they will get contaminated. You will be able to make educated selections and choose the strategy that is most appropriate for your cultivation requirements if you have a solid awareness of the several approaches, procedures, and methods that are available for pasteurization and inoculation.

Remember to constantly adopt adequate hygiene and safety precautions, experiment with new procedures, and always modify your methods to attain the greatest outcomes as you continue to learn and grow your abilities in mushroom farming. You may become a proficient and successful mushroom farmer through commitment and patience, and in doing so, you will be able to take advantage of the numerous perks and rewards that this interesting pastime has to offer.

Chapter 4: Mushroom Cultivation from Spores or Mycelium

When it comes to cultivating your own mushrooms, one of the most important aspects is learning how to cultivate them from spores or mycelium. By gaining an understanding of the many kinds of cultivation methods, such as bottle culture, bag culture, and substrate culture, you will be able to choose the approach that is most suited to meet your requirements. Growing mushrooms from spores or mycelium is the topic of discussion in this chapter. We will go over the numerous cultivation techniques, the equipment that is required, and the procedures that are involved in the process.

Spores vs. Mycelium

Before delving into the various methods of cultivation, it is vital to have a solid understanding of the distinctions between spores and mycelium, as well as their respective functions in the development of mushrooms.

Spores

Fungi, such as mushrooms, generate spores, which are reproductive cells that are very small and microscopic. They have the ability to germinate into new mycelium and are comparable to the seeds of plants. Spores are discharged from the gills, pores, or other structures of the fruiting body of a mushroom, and they may be collected and utilized to produce new mushroom cultures. Spores can also be found in the mushroom's spore print.

Mycelium

The vegetative portion of a fungus is known as the mycelium, and it is composed of a network of structures that resemble threads and are termed hyphae. It does this as it pushes its way through the substrate, decomposing organic waste and soaking up nutrients. Mycelium will only produce fruiting bodies, often known as mushrooms, in the presence of favorable environmental circumstances. Mushrooms are what we see and eat. When growing mushrooms from mycelium, you must first transplant a tiny portion of the living mycelium onto a new substrate in order to allow the fungus to spread and multiply.

Varieties of Methods Used in Cultivation

Growing mushrooms may be accomplished via a number of different growth methods, each of which has a unique set of benefits and drawbacks. Methods of growing bacteria in bottles, bags, and substrates are going to be covered in this section.

Bottle Culture

The cultivation of mushrooms via bottle culture is a well-liked technique, particularly in the context of commercial operations, due to the method's scalability and effective use of available space. Mushrooms are cultivated using this method in bottles made of transparent, reusable plastic or glass that have been filled with a substrate that has been sterilized or pasteurized. After this, the bottles are sealed and injected with mycelium or spores in order to provide a closed habitat in which the mushrooms may develop.

The following are some advantages of bottle culture:

- Effective use of space, which enables the cultivation of mushrooms at a high density
- Reusable containers, which result in less waste and lower overall costs
- An environment that is contained, hence reducing the possibility of contamination.
- It is simple to track the development and well-being of the mushrooms.

Bottle culture's drawbacks include the following:

- It's possible to have a big initial investment in equipment and bottles.
- It's possible that some types of mushrooms won't work well with this technique.
- The process of cleaning and sanitizing the bottles in between uses might be labor-intensive.

Bag Culture

Growing mushrooms using bag culture is another common approach, especially among hobbyists and home gardeners who cultivate mushrooms on a small scale. This method calls for the use of specific, permeable bags that are then stuffed with a sterilized or pasteurized substrate. After the bags have been sealed and injected with spores or mycelium, they are hung or piled in a certain location to allow the fungus to develop.

The advantages of bag culture are as follows:

- The initial investment is not very high
- Simple in both its installation and ongoing care.
- Compatible with a wide assortment of types of mushrooms
- Adaptable to both industrial and domestic settings because of its scalability.

The following are the drawbacks of the bag culture:

- Waste may be produced by using bags for single use.
- When compared to bottle culture, monitoring the development of mushrooms might be a more difficult task.
- Because of the increased surface area that is exposed to the environment, there is a greater potential for contamination.

Substrate Culture

Mushrooms may be grown using a technique known as substrate culture, which involves growing the fungi directly on a prepared substrate such as a bed of straw, wood chips, or compost. Depending on the plant species being grown and the resources that are readily accessible, this kind of cultivation may be carried out in trays, raised beds, or even directly on the ground.

The following are some advantages of substrate culture:

- It can be inexpensive and is appropriate for cultivating a broad range of mushroom species, including some that thrive best in an atmosphere that is closer to their native habitat.
- It can be readily increased or decreased in size, depending on the amount of available space and the yield that is required.

The following are some of the drawbacks of substrate culture:

- When compared to bottle or bag culture, it demands a greater amount of area.
- Because of the greater contact with the surrounding environment, there is a higher potential for contamination.
- It could need a greater amount of upkeep and monitoring, such as regular watering and temperature adjustments.

Essential Items for a Successful Mushroom Farming Operation

If you want to successfully grow mushrooms from spores or mycelium, there are several pieces of equipment that you will need to have. These fundamental pieces of equipment are not dependent on the growth technique that you choose.

Equipment Used for the Processes of Sterilization and Pasteurization

It is essential to successfully cultivate mushrooms that you keep the surrounding environment sanitary. Before inoculation, substrates, equipment, and containers may be sterilized using a variety of different pieces of apparatus, including autoclaves and pressure cookers. For pasteurization, you may use a big pot or steam pasteurization equipment.

Instruments and Supplies for Inoculation

You will need various implements, like inoculation loops, scalpels, and tweezers, in order to transfer spores or mycelium to the substrate of your choice. In order to provide a sterile setting for the inoculation process, you may also need a laminar flow hood or a still air box.

Containers

The technique of plant growth that you choose will determine the kind of container that you need to use. You'll need bottles made of transparent plastic or glass with lids in order to do bottle culture. Bag culture calls for the use of specialized bags that are air-permeable and come with filter patches. It's possible that you'll need trays, raised beds, or other containers that are capable of storing the substrate in order to conduct substrate culture.

Environmental Control Equipment

In order to cultivate mushrooms successfully, you will want apparatus that enables precise regulation of the environment's temperature, humidity, and amount of available light. This may include things like heaters, humidifiers, fans, and timers. There may also be hygrometers and thermostats involved in the monitoring of the environment.

Procedures to Follow When Growing Mushrooms from Their Spores and Mycelium

The process of growing mushrooms from spores and mycelium will be broken down into its component parts in the next portion of this article. It is important to keep in mind that the particulars may change based on the kind of mushroom you are cultivating and the technique of growth that you use.

Preparation

It is vital to carefully design and prepare your growing environment before you begin producing mushrooms. This should be done before you even start the cultivation process. This involves acquiring all of the tools, materials, and resources that are required, as well as doing research about the exact needs that are needed to cultivate the species of mushroom that you want to produce.

Pick the Kind of Mushroom You Want to Grow

To get started, choose the kind of mushroom that you wish to grow. Think about things like the desired flavor, texture, and therapeutic capabilities of the plant, as well as how easy it is to cultivate the plant and whether or not the species is suitable for the technique you want to use.

Accumulate the necessary resources and equipment.

Gather up all of the essential tools, materials, and equipment, such as apparatus for sterilization and pasteurization, instruments for inoculation, containers, and apparatus for environmental control. Additionally, acquire any necessary protective gear, like gloves, face masks, and lab coats, in order to maintain a sterile atmosphere throughout the process of cultivating the plant. This is important for maintaining a sterile environment.

Get the substrate ready to go.

Determine the mushroom species you want to grow, and then select and prepare the right substrate for them. In order to accomplish this goal, it may be necessary to combine a number of components, such as straw, wood chips, or compost, and then sterilize or pasteurize the resulting mixture in order to remove any possible contaminants.

Prepare the Cultivation Space for Plants

Create a plan for your growing environment and put it into action, making sure that you can regulate the environment's temperature, humidity, light levels, and air flow to meet the requirements of the type of mushroom you want to cultivate. This may entail putting bottles, bags, or substrate containers in a specific place, such as a grow room, greenhouse, or outdoor garden. However, the technique of culture will determine whether or not this step is required.

The immunization

After you have finished preparing your growth environment, you are ready to start the inoculation procedure. This step involves the introduction of spores or mycelium into the substrate that has been prepared in order to start the development of the fungus.

The Process of Inoculation Using Spores

In order to inoculate your substrate with mushroom spores, you will generally need to construct a spore syringe or a spore print. Both of these methods are described here. To construct a spore syringe, scrape spores from a spore print into a container that has been sterilized, add sterile water, and then pull the water that contains the spores into a sterile syringe. This process should be repeated many times. In order to inoculate the substrate, all that has to be done is to use the syringe to inject the spore-filled water into the substrate.

Establishing a Mycelium Inoculation

If you are beginning with mycelium, you will normally inoculate your substrate using agar plates, liquid culture, or grain spawn. If you are beginning with spores, you will use grain spawn. To move mycelium from one agar plate to another, cut a little piece of colonized agar with a sterile scalpel or inoculation loop and then put it on the substrate that has been previously prepared. Pour or scoop the mycelium-infused material onto the substrate, whether you are doing liquid culture or grain spawn. This method works for both.

The Incubation Period

After the mycelium has been inoculated onto the substrate, the subsequent stage is to provide the optimal circumstances for it to colonize the substrate. This stage is referred to as the incubation stage, and it needs the upkeep of certain parameters regarding temperature, humidity, and light.

Temperature Control

For optimum mycelial development, each species of mushroom has a temperature range that is most favorable for it. During the incubation period, the ideal temperature range for the vast majority of species is between 21 and 24 degrees Celsius (70- and 75 degrees Fahrenheit). Make use of heaters as well as thermostats in order to keep the environment at the ideal temperature for the species you have selected.

Regulation of Relative Humidity

It is also essential for optimal mycelial development throughout the incubation process that the appropriate amount of humidity be maintained. During this stage, the majority of mushroom species favor a humidity level ranging from 85 to 95%. In order to maintain a consistent level of humidity inside the growing environment, it is important to make use of humidifiers and hygrometers.

The Regulation of the Light

Although light is not required for the growth of the mycelium during the incubation stage of the cultivation process, it is absolutely necessary for the production of fruiting bodies later on in the process. During the period of incubation, you have the option of maintaining total darkness in the developing environment or providing a small quantity of indirect light. Be very cautious not to expose the mycelium to direct sunlight or harsh artificial light since doing so might potentially impede development or cause fruiting to occur prematurely.

Observation and Maintenance of the System

During the period of incubation, you should monitor the development of your mushroom crop on a regular basis. Examine the substrate for indications of healthy mycelial development, such as white filaments that are fluffy or cotton-like and that are spreading across the substrate. You should also be on the lookout for any symptoms of contamination, such as strange colors, aromas, or textures, which may signal the presence of hazardous bacteria, mold, or other organisms. Specifically, you should be on the lookout for any indicators of contamination that include food. In the event that you find any indicators of contamination, remove and dispose of the contaminated substrate as soon as possible so that the problem does not become more widespread.

Fruiting

When the mycelium has finished colonizing the substrate completely, it is time to begin the fruiting stage of the process. Performing this step requires modifying the ambient circumstances in order to stimulate the growth of fruiting bodies, often known as mushrooms.

Humidity Control

The normal growth of fruiting bodies requires a level of humidity that is rather high. During the fruiting period, the majority of mushroom species need a humidity level ranging from 90 to 95 percent. Maintain the usage of your humidifiers and hygrometers in order to keep the atmosphere in which your plants are developing at the optimal level of humidity.

Light Control

In contrast to the period of incubation, the presence of light is absolutely necessary for the formation of fruiting bodies. At least 12 hours a day should be spent exposing your mushrooms to a constant light source, such as natural sunlight or full-spectrum artificial light. This should be done for as long as possible. This will assist in stimulating the formation of fruiting bodies and ensuring that they develop in the correct manner.

Air Exchange

In order for good fruiting body growth to occur, enough air exchange is required. A stagnant air environment might result in poor growth and a lower yield. Utilize fans or other ventilation equipment to guarantee that clean air is continually circulated throughout the growth area. This will help you maintain appropriate air exchange, which is necessary for maintaining suitable growing conditions.

Observation and Maintenance of the System

During the fruiting stage of your mushroom cultivation, it is important to keep a close eye on how things are going. Keep an eye out for indicators of healthy growth of the fruiting body, such as the emergence of little pins or knots that will ultimately develop into fully formed mushrooms. Maintain vigilance for any symptoms of contamination, and if any are found, take appropriate action as soon as possible.

Harvesting

It is time to harvest your mushrooms after they have grown to the correct size and attained the ideal level of maturity. During harvesting, the fruiting body is normally removed from the substrate by either cutting it at the base with a sharp knife or being gently twisted and pulled away from the substrate. Handle your mushrooms with extreme care so as not to harm the fruiting bodies of the mushrooms, which are rather sensitive.

Care and Storage Following the Harvest

When you have finished collecting your mushrooms, it is very important to properly care for them and store them so that they may keep their high quality and remain fresh. Your picked mushrooms should be kept in a location that is cool, dark, and well-aired. They should also be stored, ideally in a paper bag or a container with a slightly ajar top. Plastic bags and other airtight containers and bags should be avoided because they may retain moisture, which in turn can encourage the development of mold and germs.

Growing mushrooms from spores or mycelium may be a gratifying and intriguing procedure. It provides a one-of-a-kind chance to cultivate and consume one's own fresh, gourmet mushrooms and offers a wealth of other benefits. You will have the best chance of successfully cultivating a wide range of mushroom species if you adhere to the procedures described in this chapter and keep the surrounding area sterile and under control. This will allow you to tailor the mushrooms' flavor and texture to your own culinary tastes. Always keep in mind that the unique demands and requirements of the mushroom species that you select to cultivate are the most important factors in determining the success of your mushroom growth efforts. The growth of healthy mycelium and fruiting bodies is dependent on a number of environmental factors, including temperature, humidity, light, and the makeup of the substrate. You can maximize the development of your mushrooms as well as the quantity they produce if you exercise careful control over these factors, which will result in a plentiful harvest.

If you want to further develop your knowledge and competence in the subject of mushroom farming as you acquire experience and build more confidence in your mushroom cultivation abilities, you may want to experiment with new kinds of mushrooms, different substrates, and different growing techniques. The world of mushroom growing provides an infinite number of options and chances for development and discovery, which makes it an undertaking that is both fascinating and fulfilling for novice growers as well as those who have more expertise in the field. Growing mushrooms is an interesting and engaging activity that may provide you access to fresh, flavorful mushrooms while also enhancing your knowledge of the diverse and intriguing world of fungi. You will be well-equipped to go on your own voyage of mushroom culture if you follow the instructions and advice offered in this chapter. You will be able to explore the vast and exciting domain of mushroom growth from spores or mycelium, depending on which method you choose.

PART II: Harvesting and Culinary Use of Mushrooms

Chapter 5: Signs of Mushroom Maturity

The growing of mushrooms is a fascinating and satisfying procedure that results in the harvest of delectable fungi that are also beneficial to one's health. It is of the utmost importance to be aware of when your mushrooms are ready to be harvested and to utilize the appropriate practices in order to increase the likelihood of a good and fruitful harvest. In this chapter, we will dig into the indicators of mushroom maturity and explore the optimal harvesting procedures for both rookie and expert growers. Throughout this chapter, we will focus on the signs of mushroom maturity.

Signs of Mushroom Maturity

There are many types of mushrooms, and each one reaches maturity at a unique rate and exhibits a distinct set of signs that indicate when it is ready to be harvested. It is crucial for improving production and quality to have a solid understanding of the signals of maturity that are particular to the species that you are farming. In general, there are a few universal markers that may assist you in determining when your mushrooms are ready to be harvested. These indicators can be found on the mushroom itself.

Cap Development

The formation of the cap is one of the most obvious indicators that a mushroom has reached its full maturity. The caps of mushrooms will develop into different shapes as they continue to grow and mature. It is possible that the sides of the cap may begin to flatten or curve slightly upward as the mushroom approaches maturity. This is a sign that the mushroom has many different species.

Veil Breakage

The cap of many different kinds of mushrooms is connected to the stem by a flimsy membrane that is either referred to as the partial veil or the annulus. When the mushroom has reached its full maturity, the veil will split apart, revealing a ring or skirt on the stem. This is a resounding indicator that the mushroom may now be harvested successfully. It is essential to keep in mind that not all kinds of mushrooms display veil breakdown. Because of this, it is critical that you understand the particular features of the species that you are growing.

Spore Release

When mushrooms have reached their full maturity, they will release their spores, and this may be a helpful sign for judging when they are ready to be harvested. In some species, spores may gather on the surface of the mushroom or the substrate that the mushroom is growing on, judging when they are ready to be harvested. In some species, spores may gather on the surface of the mushroom or the substrate that the mushroom is growing on. This may be visible to the naked eye. However, it is vital to harvest the mushrooms before they release an excessive number of spores. This is because excessive spore release might result in decreased air quality and the possibility of contamination inside the growing area.

Methods for the Harvesting of Mushrooms

When you have decided that your mushrooms are ready to be picked, the next step, which is the most important one, is to harvest them in the correct manner. This will guarantee that you do not do any damage to the mushrooms or their delicate fruiting bodies, reduce the possibility of infection, and keep the growing environment in good general health.

Preparing for Harvest

Gather all of the essential tools and equipment before beginning to harvest your mushrooms. This includes a pair of gloves, a sharp knife or scissors, and a clean container in which to store the gathered mushrooms after they have been collected. In order to limit the likelihood of contamination during the harvesting process, it is essential to keep the surrounding area sterile at all times.

Gentle Twisting and Pulling

Twisting and tugging the mushroom away from the substrate while doing so gently is a popular method used in the harvesting process. To do this, take hold of the mushroom towards the base of the stem, and while twisting it in either a clockwise or counterclockwise direction, apply a little amount of pressure. The mushroom ought to be able to be removed from the substrate with the barest minimum of effort. Be very cautious not to apply an excessive amount of force to the mushroom since this might cause it to shatter or get damaged.

Using a Knife or Scissors to Cut Something

A sharp knife or pair of scissors may be used in yet another method of harvesting, which entails severing the stem of the mushroom at its base. This technique is especially helpful for species that are more fragile or more likely to shatter when twisted and tugged. When harvesting the mushroom using this method, hold the cap in a gentle grip and make a clean cut at the base of the stem, as near to the substrate as you can get it, using a sterile knife or pair of scissors. This will help to avoid contamination and reduce the harm that is done to the mushroom.

Care and Storage Following the Harvest

When you have finished collecting your mushrooms, it is very important to properly care for them and store them so that they may keep their high quality and remain fresh. Your picked mushrooms should be kept in a location that is cool, dark, and well-aired. They should also be stored, ideally in a paper bag or a container with a slightly ajar top. Plastic bags and other airtight containers and bags should be avoided because they may retain moisture, which in turn can encourage the development of mold and germs.

Safety Measures to Take During the Harvest

When it comes to harvesting mushrooms, there are a few safety measures you should take to maintain the health of your growing environment and the best possible result for your output.

Sterile Environment

It is essential to maintain a sterile atmosphere throughout the process of harvesting in order to cut down on the possibility of contamination. Before touching your mushrooms, make sure your hands are clean by giving them a good scrub and putting on a fresh pair of disposable gloves. You should sterilize any instruments or equipment that you will be using, such as knives, scissors, or containers, to avoid introducing potentially dangerous bacteria, mold, or other pollutants into the environment.

Timetable for the Harvest

It is vital to time your harvest correctly in order to get the highest possible quality and production from your mushrooms. Be sure to keep a careful check on the growth of your mushrooms and make a note of any changes in the form of the cap, the veil breaking, or the discharge of spores. By keeping an eye out for these signals, you will be able to decide the best time to harvest your mushrooms, improving both the quality and quantity of the produce you get.

Exercise Caution When Working with Mushrooms

The fruiting bodies of mushrooms, as well as the mushrooms themselves, are fragile and easily destroyed if incorrectly handled. When picking mushrooms, it is important to avoid crushing or otherwise damaging them in any way. Mushrooms that have been damaged are more likely to rot quickly and are also more likely to get contaminated.

Reaping the Benefits of Several Flushes

During the course of their fruiting cycle, many different kinds of mushrooms produce several flushes, also known as harvests. Following the first harvest, the substrate may still be able to sustain the development of more mushrooms, which may result in future flushes. If you want to get the most out of your substrate, be sure to follow these guidelines:

Rest Period

After you have finished harvesting the first flush, you should give the substrate some time to rest, often between seven and ten days. As a result, the mycelium will be able to repair itself and disperse nutrients throughout the substrate, becoming ready for the subsequent flush.

Repletion of Fluids

It is possible for the moisture content of your substrate to get depleted as a result of the fruiting and harvesting processes. It is possible that you will need to rehydrate the substrate either by gently soaking it in a water bath or by spraying it with water in order to provide the ideal conditions for future flushes. Be careful not to saturate the substrate to the point that it becomes waterlogged since this might result in possible contamination.

Oversight and Maintenance of the System

Continue to check the substrate for any indications of new growth while also ensuring that the temperature, humidity, light, and air exchange conditions are optimal for the particular type of mushroom that you are cultivating. You may potentially harvest many flushes from a single substrate if you take the necessary precautions, which will allow you to get the most out of both your production and your investment.

Methods of Harvesting Requisite for Individual Species of Mushrooms

Although the broad procedures for collecting mushrooms that were discussed previously in this chapter are applicable to many different kinds of mushrooms, specific species of mushrooms each have their own traits and needs, which means that harvesting those mushrooms requires more specialized strategies. In this part, we will discuss the methods for harvesting many common kinds of mushrooms, including Agaricus bisporus (also known as the white button mushroom), Pleurotus ostreatus (often known as the oyster mushroom), and Lentinula edodes (also known as the shiitake mushroom).

Agaricus bisporus (White Button Mushroom)

The white button mushroom is one of the types of mushrooms that are farmed and eaten more than any other type. Because of the relative ease with which they can be cultivated, they are a wonderful option for novice gardeners.

When picking white button mushrooms, be sure to search for these indicators of maturity:

- As the mushroom grows, the cap will expand and take on a form that is either somewhat flattened or convex. Initially, the cap will have the shape of a dome.
- Breaking of the Veil When the veil that normally connects the cap to the stem of the mushroom starts to break, this is an unmistakable sign that the mushroom is ready to be harvested. When harvested at this time, the taste and texture will be at their very best.
- To harvest white button mushrooms, carefully grab the mushroom around the base of the stem, give it a tiny twist, and then pull it away from the substrate whilemaintaining the twist. Take care not to use an excessive amount of force since doing so might cause harm to the mushroom as well as the mycelium that is contained inside the substrate.

Pleurotus ostreatus (Oyster Mushroom)

Because of their irresistible taste, meaty consistency, and easy-to-accomplish growth needs, oyster mushrooms are another kind of fungus that is often cultivated.

When collecting oyster mushrooms, check for these indicators of maturity in the mushrooms:

- Oyster mushrooms that are mature will have a convex or slightly raised cap edge, but the core section of the cap may still be somewhat concave. The form of the cap is described as an oyster.
- Oyster mushrooms have structures that look like gills on the bottom of their caps, and these structures are where the spores are released. It is time to harvest the mushroom when you see a light dusting of spores on the surface of the mushroom or the surrounding substrate.
- When harvesting oyster mushrooms, cut them at the base of the stem, as close to the substrate as you can get, with a sharp knife or pair of scissors. This will help to avoid contamination and reduce the harm that is done to the mushroom.

Lentinula edodes (shiitake mushroom)

Shiitake mushrooms are widely appreciated both for their taste, which has been described as "rich and earthy," and for the many health advantages that they provide. They need more specific growth circumstances than white button mushrooms or oyster mushrooms, but they may be effectively developed if the right instructions are followed throughout the process.

When picking shiitake mushrooms, you should check for these indicators of maturity first:

- Shiitake mushrooms that have reached maturity will have a cap that is slightly convex and margins that have a tiny inward curl.
- The spores that are produced by shiitake mushrooms, like those produced by oyster mushrooms, emerge from the gill-like structures that are located on the underside of the cap. It is time to harvest the mushroom when you see a light dusting of spores on the surface of the mushroom or the surrounding substrate.
- When harvesting shiitake mushrooms, a sharp knife or pair of scissors should be used to cut the mushroom at the base of the stem, getting as close as possible to the substrate or wood. This will help to avoid contamination and reduce the harm that is done to the mushroom.

Common Harvesting Issues and How to Troubleshoot Them

Growing mushrooms may sometimes be difficult, and there's a chance that you'll run into problems while you're trying to harvest them. In the following paragraphs, we will go through some of the more typical harvesting issues that arise, as well as present some potential remedies to these issues.

Mushrooms that Do Not Mature or Grow at A Snail's Pace

It is possible that adverse growth circumstances, such as improper temperature, humidity, light, or air exchange, are the cause of your mushrooms failing to mature or developing more slowly than intended. Review the particular needs that are associated with the type of mushroom that you are cultivating and make any required alterations to your growing environment in order to ensure that you are providing the best possible circumstances for its development.

Cracking or Splitting of the Capsules of Mushrooms

When the humidity level in the growing environment is too low, the mushroom will lose moisture, which will cause the cap to dry up and crack or split. This will also cause the mushroom itself to lose moisture. To avoid this problem, ensure that your growing environment has suitable humidity levels and spritz the mushrooms on a regular basis to ensure that they have an acceptable amount of moisture.

Fungi that Have Been Infested by Insects or Other Pests

If you do not take early action, the harvest of your mushrooms may be endangered by various insects and other pests. If you see insects or other kinds of pests on your mushrooms or in the area where they are growing, you should remove the mushrooms that have been impacted and then take measures to get rid of the pests. This may include the employment of natural techniques of pest management, such as the introduction of insects that are beneficial to the population or the use of an organic pesticide that is permitted for use in mushroom production.

Possible Contamination with Mold or Bacteria

It is possible for the growing environment to get contaminated with mold or germs if it is not kept clean and sterile or if the substrate is allowed to become soggy. Maintaining a clean and sterile atmosphere, constantly inspecting your substrate for indications of mold or bacterial development, and avoiding overwatering your substrate are all important steps you can take to prevent infection.

Post-Harvest Handling and Storage

To ensure that the freshness, taste, and nutritional content of the mushrooms you harvest are preserved, it is vital to handle and store them in the appropriate manner. After the harvest, the best way to handle and store your mushrooms is going to be covered in this part, so stay tuned for that!

Cleaning and Preserving Mushrooms

It is essential to clean your mushrooms well after collecting them in order to eliminate any dirt, debris, or pollutants that may be present. Make use of a gentle brush or cloth, and clean the surface of the mushrooms as gently as you can. It is important to refrain from washing mushrooms under running water since doing so might cause them to get soggy and ruin both their taste and texture.

The Process of Drying Mushrooms

Drying mushrooms is a good way to preserve them since it considerably increases the amount of time they can be stored and also concentrates the taste of the mushrooms. In order to dry your mushrooms, first slice them into thin pieces that are consistent with one another, and then lay them out on a wire rack or a dehydrator pan. Dry the mushrooms at a low temperature (about 95 degrees Fahrenheit or 35 degrees

Celsius) until they are brittle and fully dry. Place the dried mushrooms in a container that can be sealed tightly and keep them in a cold, dark location.

Methods for the Storage of Fresh Mushrooms

If you want to keep your mushrooms fresh for a longer period of time, you should refrigerate them after placing them in a paper bag or a container with a slightly ajar top. Because of this, the mushrooms will be able to breathe and keep their moisture content while preventing themselves from becoming waterlogged. Depending on the kind of mushroom, fresh mushrooms generally keep for up to a week after being purchased.

You may secure a successful and abundant harvest of delectable and nutritive fungus by learning the indicators of mushroom maturity and adopting the right harvesting procedures. This will allow you to get a good supply of mushrooms. You will become more competent at identifying when your mushrooms are ready for harvest as you acquire expertise and confidence in your ability to cultivate mushrooms. Additionally, you will create your own preferred methods for harvesting mushrooms as you gain experience. Growing your own mushrooms may be a fun and fulfilling activity that also provides you with a steady supply of mushrooms that are fresh, full of taste, and beneficial to your health. You will be able to maximize the production of your mushrooms and enjoy the results of your effort if you read this chapter carefully and follow the recommendations and recommendations for best practices that are mentioned in it. You may become a proficient and effective mushroom farmer if you have patience, practice, and a sharp eye for detail. If you do this, you will be able to reap the numerous rewards of engaging in this intriguing and fruitful job.

Chapter 6: Most Commonly Cultivated Mushrooms for Gastronomy

Since ancient times, people have recognized the culinary potential as well as the health benefits of mushrooms. As a result of their vast range of tastes, textures, and nutritional profiles, they provide a sense of depth and complexity to a wide variety of foods, which has led to their widespread use as a component in a wide variety of cuisines all over the globe. In this chapter, we will investigate the edible mushrooms that are grown commercially the most, with a particular emphasis on the flavor profiles and nutritional profiles of each kind. We are going to talk about wild mushrooms that can be cultivated in addition to exotic mushrooms, which are of less common species and have distinctive tastes and textures.

Wild Cultivable Mushrooms

Mushrooms that are wild-cultivable may be found growing naturally in the wild but are also possible to cultivate in a controlled environment. It may be challenging to recreate these mushrooms' one-of-a-kind tastes and textures using commercially cultivated strains, which is one reason why people seek out wild variations of these fungi. The following are some of the most common types of wild mushrooms that may be cultivated:

Morel (Morchella spp.)

Morels are very desirable due to their honeycomb-like appearance and earthy, nutty taste. As a result, they command a premium price. They may be produced by the use of certain procedures, such as the inoculation of appropriate substrates with spores, and they are frequently discovered in forested regions, especially in the areas surrounding trees that have died or are on their way out. Morels contain a significant amount of a variety of vitamins and minerals, such as vitamin D, B vitamins, and iron.

Chanterelle (Cantharellus spp.)

The chanterelles have a beautiful golden hue, a trumpet-like form, and a delicious flavor that is similar to the smell of apricots. They are able to be grown via techniques such as the inoculation of mycorrhizal fungi on host trees and may typically be found in deciduous and coniferous woods. The fungus known as chanterelles is rich in a variety of nutrients, including vitamins, minerals, and fiber.

Porcini (Boletus edulis)

The powerful taste and meaty consistency of porcini mushrooms, which are sometimes referred to as cep or king bolete, make them very desirable. They are able to be developed via the use of mycorrhizal inoculation methods and are generally found in regions of mixed forest. Protein, B vitamins, and vital minerals such as potassium, phosphorus, and copper may all be found in high concentrations in porcini mushrooms.

Exotic Mushrooms

Exotic mushrooms are species that are not very common and provide unique tastes and textures not typically found in more readily available varieties. The novelty and culinary appeal of these mushrooms are often the motivations for their cultivation. Examples of well-known exotic mushrooms include the following:

Enoki (Flammulina velutipes)

The stems of enoki mushrooms are long and thin, and their caps are often tiny and white. Enoki mushrooms are also known as golden needle mushrooms and velvet shank mushrooms. Because of their mild, somewhat fruity taste and crisp, crunchy texture, they are often used as an ingredient in a variety of dishes, including salads, soups, and stir-fries. The antioxidants, vitamin B, and dietary fiber content of enoki mushrooms are very high.

Lion's Mane (Hericium erinaceus)

The lion's mane mushroom gets its name from its peculiar look, which is said to resemble the mane of a lion. Lion's mane mushrooms have a taste and texture that are distinctive, and they are often likened to seafood, notably crab and lobster. They are a staple ingredient in a wide range of meals, such as pasta, soups, and sautés, among others. Because they contain chemicals that may encourage nerve development and repair, lion's mane mushrooms are well-known for the possible cognitive and neurological health advantages that they may provide.

Black Trumpet (Craterellus cornucopioides)

The velvety texture and deep, smokey taste of black trumpet mushrooms, also known as the horn of plenty or black chanterelles, make them a prized component in gourmet cooking. Other names for black trumpet mushrooms are the horn of plenty and black chanterelles. They are most often found in deciduous woods and may be grown using techniques that are similar to those used in the production of chanterelles. The black trumpet mushroom is an excellent source of a variety of vitamins, minerals, and free radical-fighting antioxidants.

Shiitake (Lentinula edodes)

The meaty texture and strong umami taste of shiitake mushrooms have made them a popular crop in East Asia for ages. Shiitake mushrooms are native to that region. They are often used in Asian cuisine, notably in meals that are prepared in Japan, China, and Korea. They are well-known for the possible health advantages that they provide, including the ability to strengthen the immune system and the qualities that decrease cholesterol. The shiitake mushroom is an excellent source of a variety of vitamins, most notably B vitamins, as well as minerals like copper, manganese, and selenium.

Oyster (Pleurotus spp.)

Oyster mushrooms have a taste that is light and delicate, with a hint of sweetness, and a texture that is sensitive and velvety. They are a popular and adaptable edible fungus. They may be available in a variety of hues, including white, gray, pink, and yellow, and are often used in a vast assortment of recipes, ranging from stir-fries and soups to pasta and risotto. The nutritional profile of oyster mushrooms includes a high concentration of vitamins, in particular B vitamins, as well as critical minerals like potassium, phosphorus, and zinc.

The Flavor and the Nutritional Benefits of Edible Mushrooms

Mushrooms are highly regarded not just for the unique qualities of their tastes and textures but also for the beneficial effects they have on one's health. They are low in calories, fat, and salt, and they do not contain any cholesterol; thus, they are an excellent addition to diets that place an emphasis on health. In addition to this, mushrooms are an excellent source of a wide variety of vitamins, minerals, and other important nutrients, such as:

Vitamins

Mushrooms are a good source of the B vitamins, notably riboflavin (B2), niacin (B3), and pantothenic acid (B5), which all contribute to the maintenance of healthy brain and nervous system function as well as the creation of energy. When grown in an environment with sunshine or UV radiation, some types of mushrooms, such as maitake and shiitake, become excellent sources of vitamin D. Vitamin D is necessary for the maintenance of healthy bones and the proper operation of the immune system.

Minerals

Mushrooms are an excellent source of several different vital minerals, including zinc, copper, potassium, phosphorus, and selenium. These minerals are necessary for the body to carry out a variety of activities, including maintaining a healthy fluid balance, bone and tooth health, antioxidant protection, and immune system function.

Protein and Fiber

Mushrooms have a reasonable quantity of protein, making them an important component of plant-based diets despite the fact that their protein content is far lower than that of foods derived from animals. In addition, mushrooms are an excellent source of dietary fiber that helps with digestion and promotes healthy heart function by contributing to a reduction in blood cholesterol levels.

Antioxidants in Addition to Other Benefits to Health

Mushrooms include a variety of antioxidants, including ergothioneine, glutathione, and selenium, that help protect cells from oxidative damage and may lead to decreased inflammation as well as a lower chance of developing chronic diseases. Some mushrooms, such as shiitake and maitake, contain substances that may have the ability to enhance the immune system, while other mushrooms, such as lion's mane, may have the ability to protect the nervous system.

Growing Edible Mushrooms in the Comfort of Your Own Home

Growing your own mushrooms is a gratifying and sustainable way to enjoy the one-of-a-kind flavors and many health benefits of these culinary gems. Growing mushrooms at home not only allows you to guarantee the quality, freshness, and safety of the mushrooms, but it also allows you to reduce your impact on the environment. In this part, we are going to go over the fundamentals of growing mushrooms at home as well as some helpful hints and suggestions.

Selecting the Appropriate Species of Mushroom

When determining which kind of mushrooms to grow, it is important to take into account things like personal preferences about their taste, the growth conditions, and how easy they are to produce. Because of their ease of cultivation and versatility in response to a wide range of environmental factors, some types of mushrooms, such as oysters and shiitake, are ideal options for novice growers. Others, such as morels and truffles, may provide more of a challenge and call for the use of more specialist expertise and methods.

Choosing the Most Appropriate Cultivation Medium

To achieve their full potential, many kinds of mushrooms need particular types of substrates. Sawdust from hardwoods, straw, and grain that has been pasteurized are all common substrates used in mushroom production. It is of the utmost importance to choose the proper substrate for the type of mushroom you want to cultivate, as well as to check that the substrate is clean and devoid of any pollutants that can impede growth or lead to the formation of pathogenic molds or bacteria.

Establishing the Optimal Conditions for Plant Growth

To reach their full potential, mushrooms need a certain climate, one that provides the right balance of temperature, humidity, light, and air circulation. It is essential to study the ideal growth circumstances for the kind of mushroom you have selected and to construct a growing habitat that satisfies these prerequisites. In this case, it may be necessary to make an investment in apparatus such as humidity controls, heaters, or fans in order to keep the temperature, humidity, and airflow at optimum levels.

Inoculation and Colonization

Inoculation is the act of transferring mushroom spores or mycelium to the prepared substrate, while colonization is the process of the mycelium developing and spreading throughout the substrate. Inoculation and colonization are two different terms for the same process. In order to successfully cultivate mushrooms, it is essential to perform proper inoculation and colonization. This is because these processes guarantee that the mycelium has sufficient time to expand and mature before fruiting occurs.

The Process of Bearing Fruit and Harvesting

When the mycelium has finished colonizing the substrate completely, it will start to create fruiting bodies, sometimes known as mushrooms. Alterations in the ambient circumstances, such as a decrease in temperature, an increase in humidity, or exposure to light, are often necessary for the completion of this stage. Monitoring the growth environment on a consistent basis and making any required modifications will go a long way toward ensuring a fruitful harvest. When the mushrooms have reached their full maturity, harvest them by gently twisting them or cutting them at the base. This should be done so as not to damage the mycelium.

Common Solutions to Problems Encountered in Mushroom Cultivation

Growing mushrooms at home may present a number of difficulties similar to those encountered in any other kind of gardening venture. A prosperous and fruitful harvest may be ensured by first making sure that any possible problems are identified and then learning how to solve those problems.

Contamination

In the process of growing mushrooms, contamination by mold, bacteria, or other fungi is one of the most often encountered obstacles. To reduce the likelihood of contamination, it is important to keep the growth environment clean and sterile, to utilize substrates of high quality, and to sterilize or pasteurize the substrate in the appropriate manner before inoculating it.

Poor fruiting

Inadequate growth conditions, such as those with poor temperature, humidity, light, or air exchange, might be the cause if your mushrooms do not create fruiting bodies. It is important to conduct a thorough analysis of the growth environment and make any required alterations in order to stimulate fruiting.

Growth That Is Irregular or Sluggish

Lack of appropriate nutrients, uneven moisture distribution on the substrate, or poor air exchange may all contribute to delayed or uneven development. Making adjustments to the growing conditions and making sure that the moisture and nutrients in the substrate are distributed evenly may both encourage more consistent development.

Methods for the Preservation and Storage of Edible Mushrooms

After you have harvested your mushrooms, it is very necessary to properly preserve and store them in order to keep their taste, consistency, and nutritional characteristics intact. The following are some of the most prevalent techniques for preserving mushrooms:

Evaporation

Drying is one of the most common ways to preserve mushrooms, and it is also one of the easiest. To dry mushrooms, first, clean them well and then slice them into pieces that are uniformly thin. Place the slices in a single layer on a wire rack or drying tray, taking care that they do not come into contact with one another or overlap. You may speed up the process by using a food dehydrator, in which case you should position the rack in a place that has good ventilation, is chilly, and is dark. To ensure that the taste and consistency of the dried mushrooms are preserved, store them in an airtight container in a cold, dark location.

Freezing

Freezing mushrooms is an additional efficient method for preserving them; this method is especially useful for mushroom species that do not dry well or that lose their texture when dried. First, clean the mushrooms, and then slice or chop them into the required sizes. Then, freeze them. After giving the mushrooms a quick blanch in water that's been brought to a boil for one to two minutes, put them in an ice bath to halt the cooking process. After removing any excess liquid from the mushrooms, dry them well with a clean towel and arrange them in a single layer on a baking sheet. After the mushrooms have been frozen until they have solidified, place them in freezer bags or containers that are airtight for long-term preservation.

Putting in Cans

Canning is a way of preserving food that takes more time than other methods, but it may provide wonderful results. To preserve mushrooms, first clean and prepare them in any way you choose, and then put them into canning jars that have been sterilized. The mushrooms should be covered with boiling water, and there should be a headspace of at least half an inch at the top of the jar. After putting on the sterilized lids and rings, the jars need to be processed in a pressure canner in accordance with the instructions provided by the manufacturer as well as the appropriate processing timeframes. The canned mushrooms may be kept for up to a year in a location that is cold and dark.

Pickling

Pickling is a great method for preserving mushrooms since it brings out their distinctive taste and acidity. To make mushrooms into pickled mushrooms, first clean and prepare them in any way you choose, and then put them into canning jars that have been sterilized. Bring the ingredients for the pickling brine (vinegar, water, salt, and any desired spices or flavorings), which will be used to preserve food, to a boil. After pouring the boiling brine over the mushrooms, be sure to leave a headspace of at least half an inch at the top of the jar. Place the sterilized lids and rings on the jars, and then process them in a canner that uses a boiling water bath according to the instructions provided by the manufacturer and the appropriate processing timeframes. Keep the mushrooms in a cold, dark area for up to one year after you have pickled them.

Enjoying Your Homegrown Gastronomic Mushrooms

Growing and harvesting your own mushrooms can be an extremely satisfying experience. Mushrooms are a delectable and nutrient-dense delicacy that can be used in a wide range of cuisines. Whether you choose to eat your mushrooms fresh or preserved, including them in your culinary creations is an excellent way to enhance the taste, texture, and nutritional value of the foods you consume. Mushrooms can be enjoyed in a variety of ways.

When you grow your own mushrooms, not only do you develop a respect for the fascinating world of fungi, but you also gain an understanding of the critical function that fungi play in our ecosystems. It's possible that as you learn more about the wide variety of mushroom species and cultivation methods, you'll develop a burgeoning interest in mycology and a more profound connection to the natural world. Your forays into the world of gastronomy may get underway once you give in to the temptation to savor the tastes and get the advantages of growing your own mushrooms.

Because of their diverse range of tastes, textures, and nutritional advantages, mushrooms are regarded as one of the most valuable and adaptable ingredients in the world of cuisine. You may broaden your culinary horizons and appreciate the numerous flavorful and nutritional benefits these interesting fungi have to offer if you extend your knowledge of the many kinds of wild, cultivable, and exotic mushrooms that are out there to explore. If you are an expert chef or a home cook eager to experiment with new ingredients, the world of mushrooms provides many opportunities for the creation of meals that are not only tasty but also healthy and satiating.

Bonus Chapter: Mushroom-Based Recipes

I am delighted to welcome you to the wondrous world of mushroom-based dishes. In this chapter, we will investigate a number of mouthwatering recipes that demonstrate the adaptability and taste of edible mushrooms in a range of different applications. In this section, we will give recipes for three different types of foods: main dishes, side dishes, and desserts. As you go through these recipes, you will see how mushrooms can be used in a variety of foods in creative and delectable ways, provided they are used in the appropriate amounts. Now that we have that out of the way let's delve into the savory world of mushroom cuisine!

Main Dishes

In this part, we will introduce you to three major meals that illustrate the flexibility of mushrooms: risotto, pasta, and stew. All three of these main dishes are sure to leave your mouth watering. These recipes will show you how mushrooms can be used in conjunction with a wide variety of other ingredients to produce dinners that are both satiating and delectable.

Mushroom Risotto

Risotto is a typical Italian dish known for its velvety consistency and opulent taste. You won't be able to get enough of this mushroom and Arborio rice flavor symphony since it will leave you wanting more.

Ingredients:

- 2 cups Arborio rice
- 4 cups of vegetable or chicken broth 1 cup of dry white wine
- 1/2 cup grated Parmesan cheese
- 1/4 cup unsalted butter
- 1 big onion, cut very small and set aside.
- 3 cups mixed mushrooms (such as cremini, shiitake, and oyster), sliced 2 cloves garlic, minced
- Various amounts of salt and pepper, to taste
- To decorate, use fresh parsley that has been cut.

Instructions:

1. The broth should be brought to a simmer in a medium-sized pot and then kept warm over low heat.
2. Butter should be melted over medium heat in a big skillet or pot with a heavy bottom. After adding the onion, continue to sauté it for approximately three to four minutes or until it becomes translucent.
3. Add the mushrooms to the pan after tossing in the garlic and cooking for another minute. About five to seven minutes into the cooking process, the mushrooms should have given up their moisture and reached the appropriate degree of tenderness.
4. After adding the Arborio rice to the saucepan, give it a good swirl until all of the grains are evenly covered in the butter and mushroom combination. Cook the rice for two to three minutes or until it turns ever-so-slightly transparent.

5. After incorporating the white wine, continue cooking the rice, turning it often until the grain has absorbed all of the liquid.

6. Ladle after ladle, start pouring the heated broth into the rice while stirring constantly. Continuously stir the mixture, and once the first liquid has been absorbed, wait to add any further liquid. Continue doing this procedure for another 20–25 minutes or until the rice has reached the desired consistency of creamy and soft.

7. Take the saucepan off the stove and mix in the Parmesan cheese while it's still hot. Salt and pepper may be added to taste as a seasoning.

8. The risotto should be served hot and topped with a little fresh parsley before serving.

Nutrition Facts (per serving):

- 410 calories
- 15g fat (6g saturated fat)
- 25mg cholesterol
- 730mg sodium
- 58g carbohydrate (3g sugars, 3g fiber)
- 12g protein.

Mushroom Pasta

The earthy flavor of mushrooms, combined with the familiar consistency of pasta, makes for a meal that is both calming and tasty. The name of this meal is mushroom pasta. This dish has a velvety sauce that not only elevates the taste of the mushrooms but also creates an elegant atmosphere for eating.

Ingredients:

- 12 ounces of the kind of pasta you like most (for example, fettuccine, linguine, or pappardelle).
- 3 cups mixed mushrooms (such as cremini, shiitake, and oyster), sliced
- 2 tbsp unsalted butter
- 1 tbsp olive oil
- 1 very little onion, cut very finely
- 3 whole garlic cloves, chopped
- 1 cup of full-fat heavy cream

- 1/2 cup grated Parmesan cheese
- Various amounts of salt and pepper, to taste
- Chopped fresh parsley or basil may be used as a garnish.

Instructions:

1. Cook the pasta according to the package instructions until it has the desired al dente texture. Drain, then put it to the side.
2. Begin by melting the butter and olive oil together in a large pan set over medium heat. After adding the onion, continue to sauté it for approximately three to four minutes or until it becomes translucent.
3. After one minute of cooking with the garlic, add the mushrooms to the pan and swirl them around. About five to seven minutes later, after the mushrooms have shed their moisture and become soft, the cooking process is complete.
4. After adding the heavy cream, reduce the heat so that the mixture is just barely simmering. Continue cooking for another 5 minutes to enable the sauce to become slightly thicker.
5. After mixing in the Parmesan cheese, season the dish to taste with salt and pepper. Continue cooking for an additional two to three minutes or until the sauce reaches the consistency you prefer.
6. After the pasta has finished cooking, add it to the pan and toss it so that it is uniformly coated in the sauce.

    The spaghetti should be served hot, and it should be topped with either fresh parsley or fresh basil.

Nutrition Facts (per serving):

- 530 calories
- 23g fat (9g saturated fat)
- 95mg cholesterol
- 490mg sodium
- 61g carbohydrate (4g sugars, 4g fiber)
- 20g protein.

Mushroom Stew

A robust and tasty meal, mushroom stew showcases the meaty texture of mushrooms in a thick and savory sauce. This recipe is excellent for cold winter nights. This dish is ideal for a night spent cuddling up on the couch, and it goes well with crusty bread or mashed potatoes.

Ingredients:

- 4 cups of a variety of chopped mushrooms (including cremini, portobello, and shiitake), 2 tablespoons of olive oil
- 1 big chopped onion and 2 garlic cloves, peeled and minced
- 2 medium carrots, peeled and chopped; 2 celery stalks, peeled and chopped; 14 cups of all-purpose flour
- 4 cups of either beef or veggie broth
- 1 glass of red wine (this is optional).
- 2 tbsp. tomato paste
- 2 bay leaves
- 1 tsp. dried thyme
- Various amounts of salt and pepper, to taste
- To decorate, use fresh parsley that has been cut.

Instructions:

1. To preheat the olive oil, place it in a big saucepan or Dutch oven and set the temperature to medium. After adding the onion, carrots, and celery, continue cooking the mixture for about 5 to 6 minutes or until the veggies have become tender.
2. After stirring in the garlic and continuing to cook for one more minute, add the mushrooms to the pan. About five to seven minutes later, after the mushrooms have shed their moisture and become soft, the cooking process is complete.
3. After sprinkling the veggies and mushrooms with flour and tossing the mixture, the flour should equally cover the ingredients. Keep cooking for another two to three minutes or until the flour has a very soft golden color.

4. While stirring consistently, slowly add the broth and, if used, the red wine. Stirring often will prevent lumps from developing. Bring the mixture to a boil, and after it has reached a boil, decrease the heat so that it is just simmering.

5. Mix in the dried thyme, bay leaves, and tomato paste before serving. Salt and pepper may be added to taste as a seasoning. Keep the stew at a low simmer for thirty to forty minutes or until the veggies are cooked through, and the sauce has thickened.

6. Take the bay leaves out of the can and throw them away. Make any necessary adjustments to the seasoning.

7. The stew should be served steaming hot with a garnish of fresh chopped parsley.

Nutrition Facts (per serving):
- 280 calories
- 12g fat (3g saturated fat)
- 0mg cholesterol
- 720mg sodium
- 35g carbohydrate (8g sugars, 6g fiber)
- 9g protein.

Mushroom-Stuffed Bell Peppers

These bell peppers packed with mushrooms make for a delectable and wholesome vegetarian main dish that is ideal for a supper with fewer calories or for a special occasion.

Ingredients:
- 4 big peppers of any color in the bell pepper family
- 2 tbsp. olive oil
- 1 very little onion, cut very finely
- 2 garlic cloves, chopped or minced
- 3 cups of chopped mixed mushrooms (including cremini, shiitake, and oyster mushrooms, among others)
- 1 ounce of rice or quinoa that has been cooked
- 1 cup of shredded cheese (either mozzarella or cheddar, for example).
- 1/4 cup of fresh parsley that has been chopped

- Various amounts of salt and pepper, to taste

Instructions:

1. Prepare a temperature in your oven of 375 degrees Fahrenheit (190 degrees Celsius). Remove the seeds and ribs from the bell peppers, then cut off the tops of the peppers. Put the peppers in a different bowl.
2. The olive oil should be heated up in a big pan over medium heat. After adding the onion, continue to sauté it for approximately three to four minutes or until it has softened. Once the garlic has been added, continue to cook for an additional minute.
3. After approximately 5 to 7 minutes of cooking, stir in the chopped mushrooms and continue cooking until the mushrooms have shed their moisture and become soft.
4. After taking the pan from the heat, add the cooked quinoa or rice, along with the shredded cheese and chopped parsley, and toss to combine. Add salt and pepper to taste, and then mix everything together.
5. To ensure that the mushroom mixture is properly distributed throughout the bell peppers, stuff each one with it and then push down on them.
6. Put the filled bell peppers in a baking dish and cover with aluminum foil to keep the peppers from becoming burned. Bake the peppers for 35 to 40 minutes or until the desired softness is reached.
7. Take off the aluminum foil and continue baking for another 5 to 10 minutes or until the cheese is melted and bubbling.
8. As a delightful and filling main meal, serve the bell peppers that have mushrooms filled inside of them.

Nutrition Facts (per serving):

- 440 calories
- 22g fat (7g saturated fat)
- 92mg cholesterol
- 560mg sodium
- 17g carbohydrate (6g sugars, 1g fiber)
- 39g protein

Mushroom and Spinach Lasagna

This mushroom and spinach lasagna is a hearty and delectable main meal that highlights the earthy taste of mushrooms in a dish that is creamy and cheesy.

Ingredients:

- 12 cooked lasagna noodles, prepared in accordance with the directions on the box
- 2 tbsp. olive oil
- 1 minced clove of garlic and 1 finely chopped small onion
- 4 cups mixed mushrooms (such as cremini, shiitake, and oyster), sliced
- 4 cups of chopped fresh spinach, coarsely measured out
- 3 cups of ricotta cheese
- 2 cups of mozzarella cheese that has been shredded
- 1 cup of Parmesan cheese that has been grated
- one big egg
- 2 cups of marinara sauce
- Various amounts of salt and pepper, to taste

Instructions:

1. Prepare your oven by preheating it to 350 degrees Fahrenheit (175 degrees Celsius). Prepare a baking dish that is 9 by 13 inches (23 by 33 cm) and put it aside after greasing it.
2. The olive oil should be heated up in a big pan over medium heat. After adding the onion, continue to sauté it for approximately three to four minutes or until it has softened. Once the garlic has been added, continue to cook for a minute more.
3. After around five to seven minutes, after stirring in the sliced mushrooms, continue cooking them until they have given up their moisture and become soft. After adding the chopped spinach and cooking it for around two to three minutes, the spinach should have wilted. Add salt and pepper to taste, and then mix everything together.
4. Ricotta cheese, one cup of mozzarella cheese, half a cup of Parmesan cheese, and one egg should all be mixed together in a separate basin. Combine thoroughly.
5. When you are ready to make the lasagna, begin by coating the bottom of the prepared baking dish with a thin layer of marinara sauce. On top of the sauce, arrange a layer of lasagna noodles, then

distribute half of the ricotta mixture, then half of the mushroom and spinach combination, and finally, cover everything with another layer of marinara sauce. Repeat the layering process, beginning with a new layer of lasagna noodles, then adding the remaining ricotta mixture, then the remaining mushroom and spinach combination, and finally adding a new layer of marinara sauce. Add one more layer of lasagna noodles and the rest of the marinara sauce to the top of the dish.

6. On top of the lasagna, evenly distribute the remaining one cup of mozzarella cheese and the remaining half cup of Parmesan cheese.

7. After lining the baking dish with aluminum foil, place it in an oven that has been set to 350 degrees Fahrenheit, and bake the lasagna for 30 minutes. Take off the aluminum foil and continue baking for another 15 to 20 minutes or until the cheese is melted and bubbling.

8. Before cutting it and serving it, you should let the lasagna with mushrooms and spinach cool for at least ten minutes.

Nutrition Facts (per serving):

- 425 calories
- 22g fat (11g saturated fat)
- 65mg cholesterol
- 740mg sodium
- 35g carbohydrate (7g sugars, 3g fiber)
- 24g protein

Side Dishes

Any cuisine may benefit from the addition of mushrooms since they provide both taste and substance to the table. As a side dish, mushrooms may be prepared in a variety of ways, including grilling, sautéing, and roasting, all of which will be covered in this section. These dishes, which are simple yet tasty, will highlight the natural flavor and consistency of the mushrooms.

Grilled Mushrooms

Mushrooms, when grilled, are an excellent side dish for summertime barbecues and other outdoor get-togethers. This recipe calls for the use of a simple marinade in order to improve the flavor of the mushrooms without masking their original flavor.

Ingredients:

- 1 pound of a variety of mushrooms, whole or half, depending on their sizes, such as cremini, portobello, and shiitake
- 1/4 cup olive oil
- 3 tbsp balsamic vinegar
- 2 fresh garlic cloves, minced
- 1 tsp. dried rosemary
- Various amounts of salt and pepper, to taste

Instructions:

1. Olive oil, balsamic vinegar, minced garlic, and chopped rosemary should be mixed together in a small basin using a whisk. Salt and pepper may be added to taste as a seasoning.
2. After pouring the marinade over the mushrooms, place them in a shallow dish or a plastic bag that can be sealed, whichever you choose. Make sure that the mushrooms have a good coating. Arrange them in a shallow dish or a plastic bag that can be sealed, whichever you choose. Make sure that the mushrooms have a good coating. Marinate for a minimum of half an hour and up to two hours for a taste that is more intense.
3. Prepare the grill for cooking over medium-high heat. If you are using smaller mushrooms, thread them onto skewers, but if you are using bigger mushrooms, you may lay them right on the grill.
4. Cook the mushrooms on the grill for three to four minutes on each side or until they are soft and have a smoky flavor.
5. You can make an exquisite side dish out of the grilled mushrooms by serving them with your go-to main meal.

Nutrition Facts (per serving):

- 180 calories
- 8g fat (3g saturated fat)

- 30mg cholesterol
- 300mg sodium
- 21g carbohydrate (1g sugars, 1g fiber)
- 6g protein

Sautéed Mushrooms

Mushrooms that have been sautéed are a side dish that can be prepared quickly and easily, and they go well with many different kinds of main meals. The inherent tastes of the mushrooms are brought out with the help of a simple combination of butter and garlic, which is used in this recipe.

Ingredients:
- 1 lb mixed mushrooms (such as cremini, shiitake, and oyster), sliced;
- 2 tbsp unsalted butter
- 2 fresh garlic cloves, minced
- Various amounts of salt and pepper, to taste
- To decorate, use fresh parsley that has been cut.

Instructions:
1. Butter should be warmed over a medium heat setting in a big skillet. After about a minute of cooking, add the garlic and stir it around until it becomes aromatic.
2. Add the mushrooms to the pan and cook them over medium heat, tossing them regularly for approximately five to seven minutes or until they have given off their moisture and become soft.
3. Add more salt and pepper to taste, then top the mushrooms with them. Continue cooking for a further one to two minutes so that the flavors may combine.
4. Take the pan from the heat, and then transfer the mushrooms that have been sautéed to a serving plate.
5. Serve as a side dish, garnished with fresh chopped parsley, and enjoy.

Nutrition Facts (per serving):
- 160 calories
- 12g fat (4g saturated fat)
- 15mg cholesterol

- 260mg sodium
- 9g carbohydrate (3g sugars, 2g fiber)
- 5g protein

Roasted Mushrooms

A fragrant and gratifying side dish that needs little work to prepare, roasted mushrooms are a delicious option. The high heat of the oven helps to concentrate the flavors of the mushrooms, which results in a meal that is both decadent and mouthwateringly good.

Ingredients:

- 1 pound of assorted mushrooms, whole or half, depending on size (including cremini, shiitake, and oyster varieties),
- 3 tbsp. olive oil
- 2 fresh garlic cloves, minced
- Various amounts of salt and pepper, to taste
- Leaves of fresh thyme for use as a garnish

Instructions:

1. Prepare a baking sheet by lining it with parchment paper and preheating your oven to 425 degrees Fahrenheit (220 degrees Celsius).
2. To ensure that the mushrooms are evenly covered with olive oil and garlic, toss them in a large bowl until the basin is full. Salt and pepper may be added to taste as a seasoning.
3. Arrange the mushrooms in a single layer on the baking sheet that has been previously prepared.
4. Cook the mushrooms in an oven that has been warmed to 400 degrees for 20 to 25 minutes or until they are soft and have developed a light brown color.
5. Take the mushrooms out of the oven and place them on a plate that is intended for serving. Prepare as a side dish and garnish with fresh thyme leaves before serving.

Nutrition Facts (per serving):

- 120 calories
- 9g fat (4g saturated fat)
- 15mg cholesterol

- 280mg sodium
- 6g carbohydrate (2g sugars, 1g fiber)
- 4g protein

Garlic and Herb Stuffed Mushrooms

These garlic and herb-stuffed mushrooms are great for serving as a side dish or appetizer for a special occasion or for entertaining guests. They are both tasty and elegant.

Ingredients:

1. 24 big button mushrooms, or cremini mushrooms, washed and trimmed of their stems
2. 8 ounces of softened cream cheese
3. 1/4 cup grated Parmesan cheese
4. 2 fresh garlic cloves, minced
5. 2 tablespoons of freshly chopped parsley
6. 2 tablespoons of freshly cut chives
7. Various amounts of salt and pepper, to taste

Instructions:

1. Prepare your oven by preheating it to 350 degrees Fahrenheit (175 degrees Celsius). Prepare a baking sheet by lining it with parchment paper, then put it to the side.
2. Mix together the softened cream cheese, grated Parmesan cheese, minced garlic, chopped parsley, and chopped chives in a medium-sized bowl until the ingredients are well blended. Add salt and pepper to taste, and then mix everything together.
3. Fill each mushroom cap with a good quantity of the cream cheese mixture. You may use a small spoon or your fingers to do this. Make sure the filling is level with the top of the mushroom.
4. After placing the filled mushrooms on the prepared baking sheet, bake them in the oven that has been warmed for 20 to 25 minutes, or until the mushrooms have become soft and the filling has become a golden-brown color.
5. As a delightful main course, side dish, or appetizer, serve the mushrooms filled with garlic and herbs.

Nutrition Facts (per serving):

- 230 calories
- 18g fat (9g saturated fat)
- 90mg cholesterol
- 290mg sodium
- 9g carbohydrate (3g sugars, 1g fiber)
- 8g protein

Balsamic Glazed Mushrooms

These balsamic-glazed mushrooms are an easy side dish that packs a lot of flavors and goes great with a wide range of different main dishes.

Ingredients:

- 1 pound of assorted mushrooms, sliced in half or quarters depending on their size, including cremini, shiitake, and oyster mushrooms
- 2 tbsp. olive oil
- Various amounts of salt and pepper, to taste
- 1/4 cup balsamic vinegar
- 1 tablespoon of honey
- 1 tbsp unsalted butter

Instructions:

1. To preheat the olive oil, place it in a big pan and set the heat to medium-high. After adding the mushrooms to the pan, continue to cook them for around five to seven minutes while stirring them on a regular basis until they have given off their moisture and become soft. Add more salt and pepper to taste, then top the mushrooms with them.
2. Honey and balsamic vinegar should be mixed together in a small bowl using a whisk. After pouring the mixture over the mushrooms that have already been cooked, continue to simmer for an additional two to three minutes or until the sauce has thickened and the mushrooms are evenly covered.

3. Take the pan off the heat and mix in the unsalted butter, continuing to stir until the butter has melted and everything is incorporated. Place the mushrooms that have been coated with balsamic vinegar on a serving dish and serve them as an appetizing side dish.

Nutrition Facts (per serving):

- 140 calories
- 11g fat (3g saturated fat)
- 15mg cholesterol
- 230mg sodium
- 10g carbohydrate (6g sugars, 1g fiber)
- 3g protein

Desserts

When one thinks of desserts, mushrooms may not be the first thing that comes to mind as an ingredient, but due to their distinct tastes and textures, mushrooms can be utilized to make sweet delicacies that are both original and delectable. Both chocolate-coated mushrooms and mushroom pie are going to be discussed in this part of the article as two inventive dessert dishes that include mushrooms.

Chocolate-Coated Mushrooms

This unexpected and scrumptious delicacy mixes the earthy flavor of mushrooms with the sweetness of chocolate, resulting in a treat that is one of a kind and satisfies in its own special way.

Ingredients:

- 12–16 fresh, tiny button or cremini mushrooms, from which the stems have been removed, and the mushrooms have been washed.
- 8 oz. high-quality dark chocolate, chopped;
- 1 tbsp. coconut oil or vegetable shortening

Instructions:

1. Prepare a baking sheet by lining it with parchment paper, then put it to the side.

2. Melt the chopped chocolate together with the coconut oil or vegetable shortening in a double boiler or a heatproof dish and put it over a pot of boiling water. Stir the mixture at regular intervals to ensure that it melts evenly and completely combines.
3. Using a fork or a skewer, gently dip each mushroom into the chocolate that has been melted, making sure that the top of the mushroom is thoroughly covered in chocolate.
4. After allowing any extra chocolate to drip off, lay the chocolate-coated mushrooms on the baking sheet that has been prepared.
5. When you have finished coating all of the mushrooms in chocolate, place the baking sheet containing the mushrooms in the refrigerator for at least half an hour or until the chocolate has completely solidified and the mushrooms are ready to eat.
6. As a delightfully different dessert option, serve the mushrooms that have been covered in chocolate.

Nutrition Facts (per serving):

- 200 calories
- 13g fat (7g saturated fat)
- 5mg cholesterol
- 25mg sodium
- 20g carbohydrate (16g sugars, 2g fiber)
- 2g protein

Mushroom Pie

The mushroom pie is a unique delicacy that takes the earthy tastes of mushrooms and blends them with the sweet flavors that are often found in fruit pies. This recipe creates a one-of-a-kind and out-of-the-ordinary taste sensation for dessert by combining apples with mushrooms.

Ingredients:

- 1 pre-made pie crust (or your favorite homemade pie crust recipe)
- 2 cups of chopped mixed mushrooms (including cremini, shiitake, and oyster mushrooms) to taste
- 2 cups of apples, peeled and chopped, in total
- 1/2 cup granulated sugar
- 1/4 cup all-purpose flour
- 1 milligram of cinnamon powder

- 1/2 milligram of nutmeg powder
- 1/4 tsp salt, 1 tbsp lemon juice
- 1 tablespoon of unsalted butter, cubed into tiny pieces

Instructions:

1. Prepare a temperature in your oven of 375 degrees Fahrenheit (190 degrees Celsius).
2. Mix the chopped mushrooms, diced apples, sugar, flour, cinnamon, nutmeg, and salt in a large bowl. Add the lemon juice and stir to incorporate. Be careful to give everything a good stir to ensure that the ingredients are dispersed evenly.
3. To make the pie crust, roll it out and then put it into a pie dish that has a diameter of 9 inches (23 cm).
4. Take out any extra dough from the perimeter, then crimp it as you see fit.
5. Place the mushroom and apple mixture into the pie crust that has been previously made and smooth it out evenly. Place the little chunks of butter on top of the filling in a random pattern.
6. If you like, you may put a lattice crust or a second pie crust on top of the pie. Just be sure to punch holes in it so that the steam can escape.
7. Bake the pie in an oven that has been warmed for 45 to 55 minutes, or until the crust is a golden-brown color and the filling is bubbling.
8. Take the pie out of the oven and let it come to room temperature before cutting and serving. Because of this, the filling will be able to thicken and become more stable.

Nutrition Facts (per serving):

- 520 calories
- 31g fat (10g saturated fat)
- 75mg cholesterol
- 320mg sodium
- 55g carbohydrate (29g sugars, 4g fiber)
- 7g protein

Mushroom and Walnut Tart

This mushroom and walnut pie is a one-of-a-kind and scrumptious dessert that mixes the earthy tastes of mushrooms with the richness of walnuts and the sweetness of maple syrup. If you love mushrooms, you will like this tart.

Ingredients:

- 1 pre-made pie crust (or your favorite homemade pie crust recipe)
- 1 1/2 cups of finely chopped various mushrooms (including cremini, shiitake, and oyster varieties), including:
- 1 ounce of finely chopped walnuts
- 1/2 cup maple syrup
- 1/4 cup brown sugar
- 3 big eggs
- 1/4 cup unsalted butter, melted
- 1 teaspoon of pure vanilla extract
- 1/4 tsp salt

Instructions:

1. Prepare your oven by preheating it to 350 degrees Fahrenheit (175 degrees Celsius). The pie crust should be rolled out and then put into a tart pan with a detachable bottom that is 9 inches (23 cm) in diameter.
2. Take out any extra dough from the perimeter, then put it to the side.
3. Mix the chopped mushrooms, chopped walnuts, maple syrup, brown sugar, eggs, melted butter, vanilla essence, and salt in a large bowl until everything is evenly distributed. Be careful to give everything a good stir to ensure that the ingredients are dispersed evenly.
4. After the tart crust has been made, pour the mushroom and walnut mixture into it and smooth it out evenly.
5. Bake the tart in an oven that has been warmed for 35 to 40 minutes, or until the crust has a golden-brown color and the filling has become firm.
6. Take the tart out of the oven and place it on a wire rack to cool entirely before attempting to remove it from the pan in which it was baked.

7. As a creative and delectable alternative for dessert, serve the tart made with mushrooms and walnuts.

Nutrition Facts (per serving):

- 370 calories
- 16g fat (7g saturated fat)
- 30mg cholesterol
- 150mg sodium
- 53g carbohydrate (34g sugars, 3g fiber)
- 5g protein

Mushroom and Fig Bread Pudding

This inventive and reassuring bread pudding with mushrooms and figs mixes the earthy aromas of mushrooms with the natural sweetness of figs in a bread foundation that has been soaked in custard. The result is a unique and comfortable treat.

Ingredients:

- 6 cups of cubed day-old bread, such as brioche or challah, toasted in a pan
- 2 cups of a variety of chopped mushrooms, such as cremini, shiitake, and oyster mushrooms, finely chopped.
- 1 cup of dried figs, diced and measured out
- 4 big eggs
- 2 cups of regular milk
- 1/2 cup granulated sugar
- 1/4 cup unsalted butter, melted
- 1 teaspoon of pure vanilla extract
- 1/2 milligram of cinnamon powder
- 1/4 tsp ground nutmeg
- 1/4 tsp salt

Instructions:

1. Prepare your oven by preheating it to 350 degrees Fahrenheit (175 degrees Celsius). Prepare a baking dish that is 9 by 13 inches (23 by 33 cm) and put it aside after greasing it.
2. Combine the bread cubes, chopped mushrooms, and dried figs that have been chopped in a big bowl for mixing.
3. The eggs, milk, sugar, melted butter, vanilla extract, cinnamon, nutmeg, and salt should each be combined in their own bowl and whisked until smooth. After pouring the egg mixture over the bread mixture, give it a good toss to make sure that the bread is uniformly covered in the egg.
4. Transfer the bread pudding mixture to the baking dish that has been prepared, spreading it out evenly and gently pushing down to ensure that the bread is buried in the liquid.
5. In an oven that has been preheated to 350 degrees Fahrenheit, bake the bread pudding for 45 to 50 minutes, or until the top is golden brown and a toothpick inserted into the middle comes out clean and easy.
6. Take the bread pudding out of the oven and let it sit for a few moments so it may cool down somewhat before serving. As an original choice for dessert, try your hand at making this bread pudding with mushrooms and figs. It's fabulous!

Nutrition Facts (per serving):

- 420 calories
- 20g fat (10g saturated fat)
- 140mg cholesterol
- 340mg sodium
- 56g carbohydrate (30g sugars, 4g fiber)
- 11g protein

Chocolate and Mushroom Mousse

This decadent dessert is both inventive and exquisite; it mixes the dense, velvety texture of chocolate mousse with the earthy taste of cream that has been infused with mushrooms. The result is a chocolate and mushroom mousse. The end product is a delicious and one-of-a-kind dessert that will undoubtedly leave an impression on your visitors.

Ingredients:

- 8 ounces of premium dark chocolate, broken into pieces
- 1 1/2 cups of the thicker cream.
- 1 cup of assorted mushrooms, cut very small (such as cremini, shiitake, and oyster mushrooms).
- 4 big egg yolks
- 1/4 cup granulated sugar
- 1/2 tsp pure vanilla extract
- A little bit of salt

Instructions:

1. Dark chocolate should be melted in a heatproof dish placed over a saucepan of boiling water. The chocolate should be stirred on occasion during melting to provide a smooth and glossy finish. Take the bowl out of the pot and place it somewhere else to rest as it cools down a little.

2. Heavy cream and chopped mushrooms should be mixed together in a pot of an appropriate size. After bringing the ingredients to a low simmer over low heat, remove the saucepan from the heat and allow the liquid to steep for ten to fifteen minutes. After pushing down on the particles in the strainer to extract as much flavor as possible, pour the cream that has been infused with mushrooms into a separate basin and strain it through a fine-mesh sieve. Throw away the sediments and wait for the cream to reach room temperature before using it.

3. Whisk the egg yolks, sugar, vanilla extract, and salt together in a separate dish that is safe to use overheat. Place the bowl over a saucepan of simmering water and whisk the egg yolk mixture continually until it is thick, pale, and slightly grown in volume. This should take around five to seven minutes. Take the bowl out of the pot and place it somewhere else to rest as it cools down a little.

4. In a separate dish, beat the mushroom-infused cream until it reaches the consistency of soft peaks with a hand mixer. Blend the melted chocolate and one-third of the whipped cream together using a gentle and slow folding motion. Combine one-half of the egg yolk mixture with one-third of the remaining whipped cream, then fold in the other half of the egg yolk mixture. Last but not least, gently fold in the remaining egg yolk mixture and the remaining whipped cream into the mousse, taking care not to overmix and collapse the mixture.

5. Using a spatula, evenly distribute the chocolate and mushroom mousse among six serving glasses or ramekins. Place the mousse in the refrigerator for at least four hours, or until it has solidified and reached the desired temperature, and then cover the glasses with plastic wrap. When you are ready to serve the chocolate and mushroom mousse, take it from the refrigerator and top each portion with a dusting of cocoa powder and, if you want, a few fresh berries. Your taste buds are in for a treat with this delectable and one-of-a-kind dessert that is guaranteed to delight and astonish them.

Nutrition Facts (per serving):

- 430 calories
- 32g fat (18g saturated fat)
- 170mg cholesterol
- 100mg sodium
- 32g carbohydrate (25g sugars, 3g fiber)
- 8g protein

Keep in mind that the nutrition information that has been given is just an estimate and that the actual values may vary based on the particular components that were used, the manner of preparation, and the amount that was served. It is advised that one make use of a nutrition calculator or speak with a qualified dietitian in order to receive more information on nutrition that is more precise.

There is a diverse selection of recipes that may make use of mushrooms, ranging from savory main courses and side dishes to creative sweets. If you use mushrooms in your cooking, you'll be able to make one-of-a-kind dishes that are absolutely mouthwatering and that highlight the variety and taste of these amazing fungi. The mushroom recipes that are presented in this chapter are intended to serve as a jumping-off point for your own culinary explorations with mushrooms; nevertheless, you are encouraged to explore and come up with your own meals that use mushrooms. Have a wonderful day exploring the world of cooking with mushrooms!

PART III: Medicinal Use and Preservation of Mushrooms

Chapter 7: Mushrooms Used in Traditional Medicine

Since the beginning of traditional medicine, notably in Asian nations, people have turned to mushrooms as a natural therapy for a wide range of maladies. This practice dates back thousands of years. Mushrooms used for medical purposes are known to exhibit a wide variety of therapeutic characteristics that are beneficial to human health due to their high bioactive chemical content. In this chapter, we will dig into the intriguing world of medicinal mushrooms, exploring their culinary uses as well as their medicinal characteristics, growing methods, and cultivation strategies.

Therapeutic Properties of Medicinal Mushrooms

Because they contain a high concentration of bioactive substances such as polysaccharides, triterpenoids, phenolic compounds, and important nutrients, medicinal mushrooms provide a plethora of advantages that are beneficial to one's health. The following are some of the medical benefits most often associated with mushrooms used in traditional medicine:

- Immunomodulating: Medicinal mushrooms are well-known for their capacity to strengthen the immune system by raising the activity of natural killer cells, macrophages, and T-cells. This effect is known as immunomodulation. This immune-modulating feature helps the body fight against pathogens and minimizes the danger of infections, as well as reducing the likelihood of infections occurring.

- Anti-inflammatory: Many medicinal mushrooms include chemicals with significant anti-inflammatory actions, which may help reduce symptoms of chronic inflammation and autoimmune illnesses. These compounds are found in medicinal mushrooms because of their long history of use in traditional medicine.

- Antioxidant: Medicinal mushrooms have a high level of antioxidants, which may help neutralize free radicals, therefore lowering oxidative stress and minimizing cellular damage, both of which may contribute to aging and many chronic illnesses.

- Adaptogenic: Mushrooms that are adaptogenic assist the body in adapting to many types of stress, including physical, environmental, and emotional stress, which in turn promotes general well-being and resilience.

- Anticancer: Certain medicinal mushrooms offer anticancer characteristics that prevent the growth of cancer cells and enhance the body's natural defenses against the formation of tumors. Anticancer properties of medicinal mushrooms

- Antiviral and antibacterial: Some medicinal mushrooms have been shown to possess antiviral and antibacterial characteristics, making them effective at warding off a wide range of infectious diseases.

Cultivation of Medicinal Mushrooms

The cultivation of medicinal mushrooms is quite similar to the cultivation of culinary mushrooms; the primary distinctions lie in the type of mushrooms that are cultivated and the particular growth conditions that are necessary. Popular culinary mushrooms with medicinal capabilities, such as shiitake and maitake, are examples of some of the most well-known medicinal mushrooms. These include adaptogenic mushrooms, such as reishi and cordyceps; immune-boosting mushrooms, such as turkey tail and chaga; and medical mushrooms with names like turkey tail and chaga.

Cultivating Reishi Mushrooms

Ganoderma lucidum, more often known as reishi, is a highly regarded medicinal fungus that has a long history of use in traditional Chinese medicine. It is usual practice to culture reishi on hardwood logs, sterilized grain, or sawdust in order to take advantage of the mushroom's immune-enhancing, anti-inflammatory, and adaptogenic effects.

- Substrate preparation: Prepare the substrate by mixing hardwood sawdust with wheat bran or rice bran. To eliminate any risks of contamination, the substrate should be autoclaved or put through a pressure cooker before being used.

- Inoculation: After the substrate has been sterilized, the reishi mushroom spawn should be inoculated into it. The mycelium may be grown on grain or on agar. The inoculation bags should be sealed with a breathable filter patch so that there is room for air circulation.

- Incubation: Put the inoculation bags in a warm, dark location with a temperature between 75- and 85degrees Fahrenheit (24 and 29 degrees Celsius) for about two weeks to give the mycelium enough time to completely colonize the substrate.

- Fruiting: Once the substrate has been completely colonized, you may encourage fruiting by exposing the bags to fresh air, increased humidity (about 85–90% relative humidity), and indirect light. It takes reishi mushrooms an average of two to three months to grow their distinctive fruiting bodies, which may take the form of antlers or kidneys.

- Harvesting: Reishi mushrooms should be collected after the fruiting bodies have reached their full maturity but just before the spores have been discharged. Utilizing a sharp knife, carefully remove the fruiting bodies from the substrate, and before storing or consuming them, let them air dry.

Cultivating Cordyceps Mushrooms

Cordyceps, also known as Cordyceps militaris, is a medicinal fungus that is very valuable due to its adaptogenic, energy-boosting, and immune-enhancing qualities that it has. Cordyceps fungi have traditionally been grown by parasitizing insects; however, it is now feasible to culture them on a grain substrate that has been sterilized.

- Preparation of the Substrate: In this step, you will prepare a substrate mixture consisting of grains that have been pasteurized, such as rice or barley. To boost the nutritional content of the substrate, you may choose to use a minuscule quantity of nutritional yeast in the recipe.

- Inoculation: After the substrate has been sterilized, the cordyceps mushroom spawn should be inoculated into it. This may be done by spreading mycelium on grain or on agar. The inoculated bags or jars should be sealed with a breathable filter patch so that there is room for air circulation.
- Incubation: Place the infected bags or jars in a dark location with a temperature of 65–75°F (18–24°C) for 2-3 weeks to enable the mycelium to thoroughly colonize the substrate.
- Fruiting: Once the substrate has been completely colonized by the fungus, you may encourage fruiting by exposing the bags or jars to fresh air, greater humidity (about 85–90%), and indirect light. In most cases, it takes between four and six weeks for cordyceps mushrooms to mature into their distinctive club-shaped fruiting bodies.
- Harvesting: Cordyceps mushrooms are ready for harvesting when their fruiting bodies have reached their full maturity and grown a brilliant orange hue. Before storing or eating them, the fruiting bodies need to be removed from the substrate in a careful manner and then allowed to air dry.

Cultivating Shiitake and Maitake Mushrooms

Both shiitake (Lentinula edodes) and maitake (Grifola frondosa) are well-known gourmet mushrooms that have a variety of health benefits, including the ability to strengthen the immune system, fight cancer, and reduce cholesterol levels. On hardwood logs or sawdust substrates, they may be grown successfully for cultivation.

- Preparation of the Substrate: When cultivating logs, use freshly cut hardwood logs such as oak, beech, or maple. In order to cultivate sawdust, you will first need to make a substrate combination consisting of hardwood sawdust and a nitrogen supplement such as rice bran or wheat bran. The sawdust substrate should be sterilized by either using an autoclave or a pressure cooker in order to eliminate any possible impurities.
- Inoculation: Drill holes in the logs and introduce mushroom spawn in the form of dowels or sawdust to inoculate the logs. Wax should be used to plug up the holes to prevent the spawn from evaporating too quickly or being polluted. In order to cultivate mushrooms on sawdust, you must first disinfect the substrate and then inoculate it with mushroom spawn in the form of mycelium on grain or agar. The inoculation bags should be sealed with a breathable filter patch so that there is room for air circulation.

- Incubation: Place the infected logs in a shady, wet outdoor location, stacking them in a log cabin arrangement to allow for ventilation. In order to cultivate mushrooms on sawdust, set the infected bags in a warm, dark location with a temperature between 75- and 80degrees Fahrenheit (24 and 27 degrees Celsius) for two to three weeks. This will enable the mycelium to colonize the substrate completely.
- Fruiting: When growing logs, you may start the fruiting process by soaking the logs in cold water for a whole day or by imitating rainfall with a sprinkler system. This is done for log cultivation. In order to promote fruiting in sawdust culture, the bags must be subjected to oxygen-rich air, a higher relative humidity (about 85–90%), and indirect light. After the fruiting conditions have been established, it normally takes between one and two weeks for shiitake and maitake mushrooms to create the fruiting bodies they need.
- Harvesting: Shiitake and maitake mushrooms should be harvested when their fruiting bodies have fully formed but before their caps have completely opened. Using a sharp knife, carefully remove the mushrooms from the substrate or logs, and then let them air dry before putting them away for storage or eating them.

Culinary Preparation of Medicinal Mushrooms

In addition to their many therapeutic advantages, medicinal mushrooms may also be used in the kitchen to create a variety of recipes that are not only tasty but also packed with essential nutrients. The following is a list of suggestions and advice about the use of medicinal mushrooms in various culinary preparations:

- Stews and soups: Simmering medicinal mushrooms like reishi, shiitake, or maitake in water or broth for an extended period of time in order to extract the therapeutic elements they contain results in a foundation that is both tasty and nutritive for stews and soups.
- Stir-fries and sautés: For a delicious and nutritious stir-fry meal, sauté shiitake, maitake, or cordyceps mushrooms with a combination of vegetables and a protein source, such as tofu or chicken. Be sure to simmer the mushrooms for an adequate amount of time so that any harsh or fibrous textures are broken down, and the flavor is brought out.
- Teas and tonics: To make a medicinal mushroom tea, soak dried mushrooms, such as reishi or cordyceps, for 15 to 20 minutes in boiling water. Honey, lemon, or ginger may be added for additional taste, and this beverage can be used on a regular basis as a tonic to improve general health.

- Mushroom powder: For a nutritious boost, grind dried medicinal mushrooms into a fine powder and add them to smoothies, cereal, or baked goods.
- Capsules and tinctures: If you're looking for a more concentrated dosage of the advantages of medicinal mushrooms, one option is to take them in the form of capsules or tinctures, both of which are widely available at health food shops and may also be prepared at home.

Mushrooms used for medicinal purposes have a range of therapeutic characteristics that may be beneficial to one's health and well-being as a whole. You may harness the power of these natural healers and enjoy their benefits in both your garden and your cuisine if you have a solid grasp of the cultivation methods and culinary uses of each of these plants.

Chapter 8: Techniques for Preserving and Storing Fresh Mushrooms

It is crucial to know how to properly preserve and store fresh mushrooms after successfully producing a batch of them in order to keep their freshness, taste, and nutritional value from deteriorating over time. In this chapter, we will go through a variety of ways to preserve and store fresh mushrooms, such as drying, freezing, and the correct methods of storage to minimize degradation and contamination.

Drying Techniques for Mushrooms

Drying mushrooms not only increases the amount of time they can be stored but it also makes their taste more intense. This makes drying a common approach for mushroom preservation. When mushrooms are dried, they may retain their quality for a period of time that ranges from months to even years. The following are some methods of drying that are often used:

Air Drying

The air-drying technique of preserving mushrooms is an easy approach that is also natural, and it takes very little equipment.

- Clean the mushrooms: Gently clean the mushrooms using a gentle brush or cloth to remove any dirt or debris. It is best not to wash mushrooms since they have a propensity to absorb water, which will cause the drying process to take much longer.

- Prepare the mushrooms: Slice larger mushrooms into thin, uniform pieces to ensure even drying. Whole dried mushrooms may be obtained from smaller varieties. Take away any components that are broken or discolored.

- Arrange the mushrooms: Spread the mushrooms out on a wire rack or mesh screen so that none of them are touching. Alternatively, you might thread the mushrooms onto a rope or skewer and then hang them in a place with enough ventilation.

- Dry the mushrooms: Place the wire rack or hanging mushrooms in a warm, dry, and well-ventilated position, such as near a sunny window or in a warm room with a fan. The best temperature range for drying mushrooms in the air is between 85- and 100degrees Fahrenheit (29 and 38 degrees Celsius).

- Examine the development: The drying process may take anywhere from one to three days, depending on the size of the mushrooms and the amount of moisture they contain. Make sure the mushrooms are drying out evenly by checking on them every day. Change their order or position as necessary.

- Storing the dried mushrooms: Once the mushrooms have reached the point where they are entirely dry and brittle, keep them in a container that does not allow air to enter them in a place that is cold, dark, and dry.

Oven Drying

Drying mushrooms in an oven is a quicker approach than drying them in any other way, but it does need careful monitoring to avoid overheating and uneven drying.

- Prepare the oven by lowering the temperature as low as it can go, preferably somewhere between 130- and 150degrees Fahrenheit (54 and 65 degrees Celsius).

- In order to clean and prepare the mushrooms, you will need to follow the same methods that you used while air drying them.

- Organize the mushrooms by placing them in a single layer on a baking sheet fitted with a wire rack and ensuring that they do not come into contact with one another.
- To dry the mushrooms, place the wire rack in the oven and leave the door of the oven slightly ajar so that any excess moisture may escape. For equal drying and better circulation of air within the oven, use a fan or a fan designed specifically for use in ovens.
- The drying process may take anywhere from four to eight hours, depending on the size of the mushrooms and the amount of moisture they contain. Always keep an eye on the mushrooms to make sure they are drying out evenly and not becoming too hot.
- When it comes to storing the dried mushrooms, you should adhere to the same procedure as when you were air-drying them.

Dehydrator Drying

It's possible that using a food dehydrator is the way to dry mushrooms that's both the most effective and the most trustworthy. Dehydrators are appliances that are created for the sole purpose of drying food by maintaining a constant temperature and providing air circulation during the drying process.

- In order to clean and prepare the mushrooms, you will need to follow the same methods that you used while air drying them.
- Prepare the mushrooms by spreading them out on the trays of the dehydrator and making sure they don't come into contact with one another.
- Adjust the temperature so that it reaches around 135 degrees Fahrenheit (57 degrees Celsius), which is the optimal temperature for drying mushrooms.
- Dry the mushrooms by placing the trays in the dehydrator and allowing the mushrooms to dry for anywhere from four to twelve hours, depending on the size of the mushrooms and the amount of moisture they contain. Make sure the mushrooms are drying out evenly by checking on them on a regular basis.
- When it comes time to keep the dried mushrooms, you will want to follow the same techniques that you used while air drying them.

Freezing Techniques for Mushrooms

Freezing mushrooms is an additional approach that works well for preserving them, especially if you want to keep their texture and color intact. The following are two methods of freezing that are often used:

Blanching and Freezing

The mushrooms are blanched by being short-cooked in water that has been brought to a boil and then frozen after the procedure. The texture, color, and nutritional content of the foods are all better preserved with this procedure.

- Remove any dirt or debris from the mushrooms by gently brushing them with a soft-bristled brush or wiping them down with a soft cloth. It is best not to wash mushrooms since they have a propensity to absorb water, which will make the process of freezing them take longer.
- To prepare the mushrooms, slice or chop them into bite-sized pieces that are all the same size. Mushrooms of small size may be frozen intact.
- To blanch the mushrooms, bring a saucepan of water to a boil, then place them in the boiling water for two to three minutes. This will remove any dirt or debris from the mushrooms. Take the mushrooms out of the water that is boiling and put them, without delay, into a basin that contains water that is ice cold. This will stop the cooking process.
- After the mushrooms have cooled, drain them and pat them dry with a clean towel or some paper towels. Draining and drying the mushrooms is the next step.
- To package the mushrooms, place them in containers or freezer bags that are airtight and remove as much air from the bags or containers as you can before closing them.
- Freeze the mushrooms by keeping the pre-packaged mushrooms for up to a year in the freezer once you have frozen them.

Flash Freezing

Mushrooms may be frozen using a technique called flash freezing, which bypasses the blanching step. This method is appropriate for the preparation of more delicate mushrooms, which, if blanched, might lose their texture.

- To clean and prepare the mushrooms, use the same techniques that are used when blanching and freezing them. This will ensure that the mushrooms are clean and ready to be used.
- Prepare the mushrooms by spreading them out on a baking sheet that has been coated with parchment paper. Take care that the mushrooms do not come into contact with each other.
- Freeze the mushrooms in a flash by placing the baking sheet in the freezer for a number of hours or until the mushrooms have become completely frozen solid.

- The mushrooms should be packaged by placing them in freezer bags or containers that are airtight and then eliminating as much air as possible before closing the bags or containers.
- Freeze the mushrooms. You can keep the packed mushrooms for as long as a year if you freeze them beforehand.

Storage Tips for Fresh Mushrooms

After mushrooms have been successfully farmed, they must be stored correctly in order to prevent deterioration and contamination. The following are some guidelines to follow while preserving fresh mushrooms:

- Maintain a dry environment for the mushrooms since moisture promotes the development of mold and bacteria. It is best to refrain from washing mushrooms before storing them, and if they are wet, dry them off by patting them gently with a clean cloth or paper towel.
- Paper bags are a great storage option for fresh mushrooms; just place them in a paper bag or wrap them in a paper towel that has been well-cleaned and dried. The mushrooms are able to breathe more easily and can better absorb any extra moisture when the paper is used.
- Avoid using plastic bags since they tend to retain moisture, which may cause food to go bad. If you absolutely have to use a plastic bag, be sure to leave a small hole or two in it so that air may circulate within.
- Mushrooms should be kept in the refrigerator. Fresh mushrooms should be stored in the refrigerator, preferably in the crisper drawer, which provides a more stable environment in terms of temperature and humidity.
- When mushrooms are kept, they should be checked on a regular basis for signs of spoiling, such as sliminess, strange aromas, or the formation of mold. Throw away any mushrooms that are showing symptoms of spoilage.

If you follow these steps for preserving and storing fresh mushrooms, you will be able to reap the benefits of your labor in mushroom gardening for a much longer period of time. Maintaining the freshness, taste, and nutritional content of your mushrooms via appropriate techniques of preservation and storage helps to ensure that you may continue to enjoy them in a variety of culinary applications or share them with family and friends.

Storing Dried Mushrooms

As long as they are kept in the appropriate conditions, dried mushrooms may maintain their high quality for an extended period of time in storage. Here are some guidelines for keeping dried mushrooms:

- Utilize containers that are airtight. To store dried mushrooms, you should use containers that are airtight, such as glass jars, plastic containers with lids that fit tightly, or plastic bags that can be resealed. Keeping the mushrooms in an airtight container protects them from collecting moisture, which may result in rotting or the formation of mold.

- Maintain a cold and dark environment for the mushrooms. Dried mushrooms should be kept in a cool, dark location such as a cupboard, drawer, or pantry. Over time, the mushrooms may see a decline in both their taste and their nutritional value if they are subjected to light and heat.

- Label and date the containers, indicating both the kind of mushroom that was used and the date that it was dried. This information will assist you in keeping track of your mushroom supply and ensuring that the mushrooms with the longest expiration dates are used first.

- Check for symptoms of deterioration: Dried mushrooms should be checked on a regular basis for any signs of spoilage, such as the development of mold, an unpleasant odor, or the presence of insects. Throw away any mushrooms that are showing symptoms of spoilage.

If you follow these preservation instructions, you will be able to maintain the tasty freshness of your dried mushrooms for months or even years.

Storing Frozen Mushrooms

Mushrooms that have been frozen may be kept for a long time; nevertheless, it is vital to store them correctly in order to keep their quality intact. The following are some suggestions for the proper storage of frozen mushrooms:

- Make use of packaging that is airtight and store frozen mushrooms in freezer bags or containers that are airtight, making sure to remove as much air as possible before closing. This helps to avoid freezer burn and prevents additional tastes from being absorbed by the mushrooms when they are stored in the freezer.

- Mark the packets with the kind of mushroom included within as well as the date that it was frozen, then date each of the marked parcels. This information will assist you in keeping track of your mushroom supply and ensuring that the mushrooms with the longest expiration dates are used first.

- Maintain them in a freezer that is well organized to avoid crushing or otherwise damaging them. Frozen mushrooms should be kept in a freezer that is well organized to avoid being crushed or otherwise damaged. Protect them from the other goods in the freezer by putting them in an area that is specifically allocated for them or by using a container that can be frozen.
- When you are ready to use the frozen mushrooms, thaw them in the refrigerator or by putting the sealed package in a basin of cold water. This should be done when the mushrooms have been frozen. It is best to avoid thawing the mushrooms in warm water or in the microwave since doing so might lead to an uneven thawing process as well as a loss of texture in the mushrooms.

If you follow these guidelines for storing your frozen mushrooms, you will be able to preserve them in excellent condition for up to a year. Frozen mushrooms, provided they are properly kept and thawed, may be used in a variety of cooking applications; this provides you with the opportunity to enjoy the results of your mushroom growing efforts throughout the whole year.

Anyone interested in growing their own mushrooms really needs to familiarize themselves with the myriad of methods available for preserving and storing fresh mushrooms. You will be able to reap the rewards of your cultivation efforts and enjoy the distinctive tastes, textures, and nutritional qualities of mushrooms in a variety of culinary applications if you follow the procedures provided in this chapter and put them into practice. Not only does proper storage assure the quality and safety of your mushrooms, but it also gives you the opportunity to show off your abilities as a mushroom farmer by allowing you to enjoy the fruits of your work with friends and family.

Conclusion

As we come to the conclusion of our adventure through *The Art of Mushroom Cultivation*, it is essential to review the information that we have acquired and to reflect on the potential of mushrooms in the fields of cuisine and medicine. We have covered a lot of ground in our extensive guide to mushroom growing. Our goal was to make sure that novices were well-equipped with the knowledge they needed to get started cultivating their own mushrooms.

In the introduction, we emphasized the cultivation of mushrooms, their usage in dish preparation, their nutritional worth, and their medicinal capabilities. Mushrooms are important not only in the culinary world but also in the medical world. This created a strong basis for understanding the importance of mushrooms as well as the possible advantages of growing them.

In the first chapter, we discussed the many kinds of mushrooms, how to identify them, and the features they have. We went through how to discern edible and hazardous mushrooms, guaranteeing that growers will be able to differentiate between the two in a way that is both safe and confident. This information is very necessary in order to ensure the security and success of any project involving the growth of mushrooms.

In the second chapter, we looked at the several substrates that may be used for mushroom growing as well as the ideal environmental factors, such as humidity, temperature, and light, that are necessary for each species. We also went through the various methods of mushroom culture, which provided novice growers with the knowledge they needed to create a healthy environment for mushroom growth.

In Chapter 3, we discussed the ideas of sterilization and inoculation, going into depth about the typical procedures that are used for each procedure. These vital measures are very necessary in order to encourage the development of mushrooms that are healthy and free of contaminants.

Chapter 4 concentrated on mushroom production from spores or mycelium, addressing the many kinds of culture techniques and the equipment necessary. These instructions are very necessary for anybody who wants to grow mushrooms at home or on a larger scale for commercial purposes.

In Chapter 5, we discussed the numerous strategies for harvesting mushrooms as well as the indicators that indicate when they are ready to be picked. We stressed how important it is to recognize when mushrooms are ready to be picked and the steps to take to ensure that they are not harmed in any way throughout the process of harvesting them.

In the previous chapter, "Chapter 6: Mushrooms," we dove into the flavor profiles as well as the nutritional profiles of the most widely farmed mushrooms for culinary use. We hoped that by drawing attention to the singular aromas and mouthfeels of these mushrooms, we might encourage and inspire readers to experiment with the myriad culinary applications of their own cultivated mushrooms.

Chapter 7 looked at mushrooms used in traditional medicine, describing their therapeutic effects as well as the production of medicinal mushrooms such as adaptogenic mushrooms, immune mushrooms, shiitake, and maitake. We also went through the many ways in which these potent fungi may be used in the kitchen, which is just one example of the variety of applications that are possible with them.

In the last chapter, we covered ways for preserving and storing fresh mushrooms, including drying and freezing procedures. These methods were discussed in Chapter 8. For the purpose of preserving the quality and safety of grown mushrooms and ensuring that they may be enjoyed to the maximum extent possible, it is vital that they be stored in an appropriate manner.

When we look to the future of mushroom production, we may predict developments in the medical field as well as advances in the food industry. As more information about the advantages and prospective uses of mushrooms is uncovered through study, the potential role that mushrooms might play in various spheres keeps growing. We have high hopes that this book has not only laid a strong foundation for novices but also sparked a deeper appreciation for, and a sense of wonder towards, the amazing world of mushrooms.

In summation, *The Art of Mushroom Cultivation* is a detailed book that attempts to provide budding mushroom farmers with more control over their growing experience as well as more information. We hope that by offering critical information on many areas of mushroom production, our readers will be inspired to explore the fascinating world of mushrooms and to take advantage of the myriad advantages that they have to offer. As we look to the future of mushrooms growing, there is really infinite potential for expansion and innovation in the fields of both cuisine and medicine.

Printed in Great Britain
by Amazon